HEART BLOSSOMS

A Commentary and Analysis
of the Exalted Mahayana
Sutra on the Profound
Perfection of Wisdom
called the Heart Sutra

S. R. Allen

ISBN 's
978-0-9887067-3-6 (Hardcover)
978-0-9887067-5-0 (Paperback)
978-0-9887067-4-3 (e-book)

U.S. Copyright Office Registration: Txu 1-868-981
 Allen, S. R.
Heart Blossoms   A Commentary and Analysis of the Exalted Mahayana Sutra on the Profound Perfection of Wisdom called the Heart Sutra
Includes Index. Sutrapitaka. Prajnaparamita.
Prajnaparamitahridayasutra.
English. 2013
BQ.........294.3

GNOSTIKO LLP
PUBLISHING

Dedicated in memory of
Ani Sangmo

CONTENTS

The Commentaries

PREFACE

It seems necessary to record here a few thoughts about what I have tried to accomplish by writing this commentary on a famous Buddhist sutra about which volumes have already been written, each with its own particular perspective or bias. Any kinds of comments may be made on any subject colored with personal bias according to whatever opinion or perspective a particular writer might have. In this work I have tried to eclipse all bias and point out the few easily overlooked ideas contained in the Heart Sutra itself. Of course, any idea or statement from any source can be interpreted with bias consonant with the degree of clarity or with the degree of delusion of whomever is writing or of whomever is reading.

In stark contrast to all the opinionated interpretations that pervade all aspects of our human condition, whether in politics, in social collaborations, in philosophy, in religion, or in anything else, this Heart Sutra is perfectly unyielding in its instructions pertaining to the necessity of getting beyond the obscuring effects of any sort of discriminative bias and showing us the way to learn how to clearly see the real truth. It is only the truth that can deliver us from our discontent.

It may be that the one redeeming quality of humankind is its discontentedness. Beyond the basic will-to-survive is an insatiable longing to *know*, and throughout human history this longing is the base motivation for all serious investigations concerned with pursuing knowledge and finding real answers to the perennial questions of philosophy, science, and religion. In the end, with all the scriptures underlined and all the sermons reiterated and grown old, uncertainty still remains and discontent persists just like a magnified shadow that follows along with us every day of our lives. The unknown something that no finger can definitely point to, that no intellectual analysis can seem to penetrate, and that no faith or surrender can fully rely upon – whatever it is that seems to be missing – that something persists in remaining missing. Even as I write this, the world we live in seems to be still searching for solutions to the most simple problems, always in a process of making some sort of "adjustment". Eighty countries and a thousand cities are undergoing demonstrations, riots, and breakdowns. It is as if someone has pushed a collective reset button. "Enough of this unnecessary suffering," people seem to be saying. Yet how much positive change can or will come if those who suffer do not know of the real *origin* of suffering? Only by eliminating the originating factors that produce suffering can relief be found.

The basic cause and condition for what remains missing and for what subsequently goes wrong is our sense-based mind, that which maintains ignorance. However, no one need live a life saddled and constrained by ignorance and its consequential actions. So it is crucial to *know*. An awakened understanding of the true state of *being* allows freedom to anyone who is willing to *see*. Knowledge releases one from the bonds of ignorance and obsessions based on a false notion of *self and other*. An integrated, dynamic consciousness is a necessity for knowing the real situation of the human condition, whether individually or collectively. It is just this kind of awareness about which the Heart Sutra instructs. Without this kind of mature truth-vision we seem to wander perpetually in an automated chaos of our own making.

The explicit aim of Buddhism in its higher reaches, which the Heart Sutra represents, is the rediscovery (or recovery) of what we really are, and of knowing with certainty what everything else really is. The task of the Sutra is to reveal this to us. To remain in the common state of non-understanding is to miss the boat, or to end up carrying the boat around with us hoping to find a little more water some place else on which we might float it again for further searching. The way of understanding is the way the Heart Sutra identifies as the clear way, a path well-marked when mind is allowed freedom from delusional bias, opinion, and expectation.

With the intent to expose more of the practical aspects of the way of bodhi as articulated in this luminous sutra, this commentary is offered to those who might find it of interest. I apologize for my many shortcomings that may have limited the clear expression of what is so difficult to clearly express with words, but trust that the approach herein outlined may serve in promoting a fuller vision of the way things really are.

_____The Author, July 2011

INTRODUCTION

The Heart Sutra is the shortest sutra in the Mahayana Buddhist collection of writings known as *Prajnaparamita*. There are about forty of these sutras still extant in the Sanskrit language in approximately six hundred volumes. The Prajnaparamita Sutra are all intimately related to each other because of the similarity of emphasis they put on the realization of awakening through the blossoming of *prajna* (supreme, unequaled wisdom), and how this process is essential to the activities of the bodhisattva idealism revealed and explained in Mahayana Buddhism.

The Prajnaparamita texts belong to the genre of Buddhist writings called *Vaipulya*, scriptures originally written down in the Sanskrit language. But over time many of them have been preserved only in Tibetan or Chinese translations. These sutras were the first Mahayana scriptures to have become widely available in India. The records of their emergence date to around 100 B.C.E., about four hundred years after the Buddha's passing. The Prajnaparamita Sutras are the most extensive and voluminous of all the Mahayana Sutras and are somewhat similar in structure to the earlier Pali Suttas in their method of teaching and in the treatment of subject matter.

Some of the most reliable scholars of Buddhism posit that unknown Buddhists groups composed the Mahayana Sutras directly from records of the teachings of the Buddha. The old legends tell us that these texts were wisely hidden away by mysterious beings called *nagas* until humankind could achieve a higher ethics and morality suitable to receive such knowledge in an appropriate fashion. The Mahayana writings were then first introduced and confined to India by a monk named Nagarjuna. The Buddha had previously said that such a one would be born in the southern part of India about four hundred years later on, and that he would bear the name of the dragon. In Sanskrit the word for a "dragon in human form" is naga.

Nagarjuna had given a discourse at the Nalanda Monastery and was there told by nagas that they had kept vital sutras safe in their undersea city, and that these would be available for him to study. And study them he did – for about fifty years – and then he took them and made them public in India. Later on Nagarjuna wrote many commentaries on subjects of the Mahayana,

the most highly regarded being his
Mulamadhyamakakarika, or "Root Verses of the
Middle Way", an abstract exposition on the premier
Mahayana doctrine of emptiness. This became a
core text of the later Madhyamaka School that
Nagarjuna founded. Nagarjuna is said to have also
discovered other texts concealed in towers and other
places, and to have lived for more than six hundred
years.

The Prajnaparamita Sutras consistently
maintain a determined focus on the doctrine of
emptiness (*sunyata*), or the absence of any inherent
or substantial self-existence of things. A Buddhist
contemplative practitioner, by way of a
progressively deeper understanding of emptiness, is
then enabled to manifest prajna-wisdom as a
bodhisattva on the Mahayana Path. The
Prajnaparamita Sutras extensively use an abstract
verbal methodology that is effective in promoting
deep understanding in a student of these writings.
This method induces the transcendence of the
conditional and habitual verbal structures of a
deluded individual mind-stream. This helps the
contemplative to deconstruct his errant formats of
perception and ideas that usually obstruct or hinder
the realization of deeper insights. The
Prajnaparamita, or Perfection of Wisdom Sutras,
extensively describe in many detailed ways, both
simple and complex, the proper way in which

emptiness should be contemplated and understood in order that awakening (*bodhi*) can occur.

Most students of Buddhism will probably have come across a famous statement concerning emptiness that comes from the Heart Sutra itself: "*. . .form is none other than emptiness and emptiness is none other than form. Form is emptiness and emptiness is form.*" This somewhat mysterious statement will be clarified further on, and it is just this emptiness doctrine that imparts the highest wisdom. It is widely agreed that only the Buddha taught emptiness, and it is found not just in Mahayana writings, but also in Pali scriptures, though with less emphasis there. The Prajnaparamita texts are essentially concerned with instructions for bodhisattvas who, through deep insight into emptiness, will correctly practice and perfect their skill in the six perfections (*paramitas*). This idea marks the beginning of the "second turning of the wheel" of the Buddha's teachings (*dharmacakraparivartana*) starting with the Prajnaparamita Sutras. The Pali scriptures containing the "Three Baskets" of the writings (*tripitaka*) represent the "first turning of the wheel". In Pali these are the *Vinaya Pitaka*, or rules of conduct for monks and nuns, the *Sutta Pitaka*, which are the recorded discourses of the Buddha, and finally the *Abhidamma Pitaka* which is the advanced and very detailed philosophical

4

psychology of Buddhism. The second turning presents a somewhat contrasting approach in the elucidation of the Two Truths compared with that of the fist turning. These Two Truths are the relative truth (*samvritisatya*) and the ultimate truth (*paramarthasatya*), the meanings of which will be addressed in a later section of this commentary.

In the first turning there were those who were having some difficulty overcoming their conditioned tendencies to regard things as ultimately real, so the Buddha began to expound the deeper implications and meanings of emptiness to them, and thus began the second turning which also depicts quite a contrast between the arhat of the Pali Suttas and the bodhisattva of the Mahayana Sutras. The main purpose of the second turning is to further reveal the truth about the realities of existence by means of the thorough exposition on emptiness, which in turn reveals the obvious necessity of the paramitas by which the bodisattvas endeavor to move toward perfection and help others along the way. The third turning of the wheel is represented by the rest of the Mahayana Sutras which also reveal aspects of emptiness as well as explaining such doctrines as the buddha-nature (*tathagatagarbha*), the mind doctrine (*cittamatra*), the three natures (*trisvabhava*), and other aspects of the Buddhadharma that complete and round out the Buddha's highest teachings.

In the generations since the Buddha began to elucidate the dharma there has been an unending effort to probe into the essence of these teachings. Since the Heart Sutra first appeared there have been numerous commentaries written on it by some of the most scholarly Buddhist teachers using widely divergent approaches. Among the most well-known commentaries are those written by Atisa, Jnanamitra, Kamalasila, Prasastrasena, Srisimha, Vajrapani, and Vimalamitra, all of India. From China, Fa-Tsang and Kukai stand out. From Tibetan tradition, Tendar Larampa, Kenchog Gromne, and the present Fourteenth Dalai Lama have produced noteworthy explanations. Japan had Hakuin and several others. Today we find interest in the Heart Sutra has not waned at all and many volumes may be found which are written on it in recent decades. Most of the commentaries, both past and recent, are written with the idea that the Heart Sutra presents a concise and mature formula which condenses the fundamental Prajnaparamita doctrines in a valuable and useful way. The Heart Sutra seems to be the centerpiece of the vast corpus of Prajnaparamita Sutras, hence its title, "Heart" (*hridaya*), meaning center, essence, or basis. Since this Heart Sutra is such a centerpiece of the Mahayana emptiness doctrine, it seems auspicious to entitle this commentary according to the way this

6

wisdom blossoms in the contemplative practitioner from his/her own real essence.

Several commentators have equated the sections of the Heart Sutra with the progressive Five Paths of Buddhahood. These Five Paths are the Path of Accumulation, Preparation, Vision, Meditation, and No More Learning. Although there are undeniable similarities in the structure of the Heart Sutra with these Five Paths, nowhere within the Sutra itself are they specifically mentioned. There are also many other subjects covered in the Prajnaparamita Sutras that are not mentioned in the Heart Sutra, so when past commentators suggest that the Heart Sutra is a condensation of all the Prajnaparamita Sutras, it must perhaps be understood as qualifiedly and relatively true. Nevertheless, the subject with which the Heart Sutra is most concerned is the correct way to perceive emptiness and to incorporate that view and realization into daily experience.

A detailed curriculum of systematized and detailed instruction was developed by Mahayana monastic organizations based on the format and formulas of Nagarjuna. The students studied the texts assiduously and heard discourses upon them. Then they reviewed and thoughtfully reflected on them and learned how to debate over the wisdom contained in the sutras and commentaries. Next, in meditation they learned to apply the knowledge they had gained. Further on it will be shown how the Heart Sutra indicates and encapsulates this same systematic procedure of study, reflection, and meditation.

Upon rising from the samadhi "perception of the profound", mentioned in the Heart Sutra prologue, the practitioner can, like the Buddha, clearly understand reality and existence and experience in a practical and perfectly holistic way instead of in the usual narrow perspective of automated, preconditioned egotistic delusion. Then there can be a blossoming of prajna revealing bodhi, the awakening that gives freedom and creative potential for the liberation of all beings.

The Heart Sutra is found in both a longer and in a shorter version. This commentary refers mostly to the longer version, but both versions are substantially the same except for two differences. The first difference is that the shorter version excludes a prologue and an epilogue found in the longer versions. The second difference is that the shorter version, in some translations, adds a line in the first section, *thus he overcame all ills and suffering.* The shorter version is found with and without this line. The only other differences between any versions must be attributed to previous translators of the Sutra who may have included or excluded a word, or of other translators who have used a clarifying creativity in their presentations. The shorter version has been chanted in monasteries, temples, congregations, homes, and gatherings of Buddhists daily for fifteen hundred years or more. It is held dear and esteemed with great loyalty and persistent devotion, memorized and chanted worldwide in many diverse languages still today.

The Heart Sutra is usually divided into sections by most commentators. The sections in this commentary are called The Title, The Prologue, The Question and the Answer, The Negations, The Mantra, and The Epilogue. These sections are easily discerned in a casual reading of the Sutra. The following are English language readings of the longer and shorter versions.

HEART SUTRA   (Long Version)

Arya Bhagavati Prajnaparamitahridayasutra

Thus did I hear at one time.

The Conqueror was sitting on Vulture Mountain in Rajagriha with a great gathering of monks and a great gathering of bodhisattvas. At that time the Conqueror was absorbed in a samadhi on the enumerations of phenomena called "perception of the profound". Also at that time the Bodhisattva, the Mahasattva Avalokitesvara was contemplating the deep meaning of the Profound Perfection of Wisdom and he saw that the five skandhas were all empty of inherent existence.

Then, by the power of the Buddha, the Venerable Sariputra said this to the Bodhisattva, the Mahasattva Avalokitesvara, "How should those of good lineage train, who wish to practice the Profound Perfection of Wisdom?"

The Bodhisattva, the Mahasattva Avalokitesvara said to the Venerable Sariputra, "Sariputra, sons and daughters of good lineage who wish to practice the Profound Perfection of Wisdom

11

should view things in this way: they should correctly view the five skandhas also as empty of inherent existence."

"O, Sariputra, form is none other than emptiness and emptiness is none other than form. Form is emptiness and emptiness is form. The same is true for feelings, perceptions, mental formations, and consciousness. Sariputra, all phenomena are characteristically empty, not created nor destroyed, neither tainted nor pure, without increase or decrease."

"Therefore, Sariputra, in emptiness there are no forms, no feelings, no perceptions, no mental formations, no consciousness; no eyes, no ears, no nose, no tongue, no body, no mind; no form, no sound, no odor, no taste, no touch, no object of mind. There is no realm of eyes and so forth up to and including no mind consciousness. There is no ignorance and no extinction of ignorance and so forth up to and including no ageing and no death and also no extinction of ageing and death. There is no suffering, no origin, no cessation, and no path. There is no wisdom and no attainment, with nothing to attain."

"Therefore, Sariputra, because bodhisattvas have nothing to attain, they rely on abiding in the Profound Perfection of Wisdom without mental hindrances. Because their minds are without hindrances they are without fear. Having passed completely beyond all errors they realize ultimate *nirvana*. All the buddhas of the three times have fully awakened into unsurpassed, complete enlightenment through relying on the Profound Perfection of Wisdom."

"Therefore, the mantra of the Profound Perfection of Wisdom is the great mantra, the mantra of great knowledge, the unsurpassed mantra, the incomparable mantra, the mantra which thoroughly allays all suffering without fail. Because it is not false it is known as true. Hence, the mantra of the Profound Perfection of Wisdom is stated as

Tadyatha om gate gate paragate parasamgate bodhi svaha!

"Sariputra, bodhisattva mahasattvas should train in the Profound Perfection of Wisdom in just this way."

13

Then the Conqueror rose from that samadhi and said to the Bodhisattva, the Mahasattva Avalokitesvara, "Well done, well done, well done, child of good lineage; it is just that way. The Profound Perfection of Wisdom should be practiced just as you have just taught it. Even the Tathagatas admire this." The Conqueror, having thus spoken, the Venerable Sariputra, the Bodhisattva, the Mahasattva Avalokitesvara, all those gathered, and all those of the world, the gods, humans, demigods, and the gandharvas were filled with admiration and they all praised the Conqueror's words.

HEART SUTRA   (Short Version)

Arya Bhagavati Prajnaparamitahridayasutra

The Bodhisattva, the Mahasattva Avalokitesvara was contemplating the deep meaning of the Profound Perfection of Wisdom and he saw that the five skandhas were all empty of inherent existence; thus he overcame all ills and suffering.

"O, Sariputra, form is none other than emptiness and emptiness is none other than form. Form is emptiness and emptiness is form. The same is true for feelings, perceptions, mental formations, and consciousness. Sariputra, all phenomena are characteristically empty, not created nor destroyed, neither tainted nor pure, without increase or decrease."

"Therefore, Sariputra, in emptiness there are no forms, no feelings, no perceptions, no mental formations, no consciousness; no eyes, no ears, no nose, no tongue, no body, no mind; no form, no sound, no odor, no taste, no touch, no object of mind. There is no realm of eyes and so forth up to and including no mind consciousness. There is no ignorance and no extinction of ignorance and so forth up to and including no ageing and no death and also no extinction of ageing and death. There is no suffering, no origin, no cessation, and no path. There is no wisdom and no attainment, with nothing to attain."

"Therefore, Sariputra, because bodhisattvas have nothing to attain, they rely on abiding in the Profound Perfection of Wisdom without mental hindrances. Because their minds are without hindrances they are without fear. Having passed completely beyond all errors they realize ultimate nirvana. All the buddhas of the three times have fully awakened into unsurpassed, complete enlightenment through relying on the Profound Perfection of Wisdom."

"Therefore, the mantra of the Profound Perfection of Wisdom is the great mantra, the mantra of great knowledge, the unsurpassed mantra, the incomparable mantra, the mantra which thoroughly allays all suffering without fail. Because it is not false it is known as true. Hence, the mantra of the Profound Perfection of Wisdom is stated as

Tadyatha om gate gate paragate parasamgate bodhi svaha!

"Sariputra, bodhisattva mahasattvas should train in the Profound Perfection of Wisdom in just this way."

CHAPTER 1

STUDY

The Arising of Srutamayiprajna

**NAMO BUDDHADHARMASANGHAYA AND
HOMAGE TO ALL THE WARRIOR SAINTS
AND ENLIGHTENED BEINGS OF THE
THREE TIMES. PEACE TO ALL BEINGS.**

In the vast and deep dharma ocean
Of the Buddha's glorious teachings
There is a tiny droplet, Heart Sutra,
Which exposes the wisdom of the profound.
Examining this droplet diligently
It is found equal to the whole ocean.
By contemplating its deep meaning
We study attentively for great knowledge.
By training thoughtfully in the correct view
We reflect on our conceptual errors.
In practicing the Profound Perfection of Wisdom
We meditate for calm and insight.
Understanding then with certainty
We transcend all mental hindrance
And through heightened full awareness
We experience the blossoming of prajna
And abide in the dharma ocean of truth,
Free and filled with admiration
For the Sutra's profound words.

This short poem introduces this monograph and refers to a five-phase progression in the way prajna blossoms into bodhi. This is given in the text of the Heart Sutra itself and is inherent in its format:

The first clue revealing the sutra's hidden structure is, . . . *Avalokitesvara was contemplating the deep meaning of the Profound Perfection of Wisdom. . . .* Here the word *contemplating* refers to study (*sruti*). This study is covered in Chapter One of this commentary.

The second in the progression is *"How should those of good lineage train, who wish to practice the Profound Perfection of Wisdom?"* In this case the word *train* refers to thoughtful reflection or critical analysis (*cinta*), a deeper level of study that deeply impresses upon the memory and understanding. *Training,* or thoughtful reflection is covered in Chapter Eight of this commentary.

The third step mentioned is *" . . .who wish to practice. . . ."* The word *practice* refers to the practice of meditation (*bhavana*). These first three steps, sruti, cinta and bhavana are descriptive of the *three root prajnas* (*mulaprajnas*) of

18

Mahayana Buddhism, *srutamayiprajna, cintamayiprajna*, and *bhavanamayiprajna.* These are related to the methodology of the Prajnaparamita Sutras. Bhavana is the subject of Chapter Nine.

The fourth clue is *"Having passed completely beyond all errors they realize ultimate nirvana."* Someone who has reached this stage is certain of having passed completely beyond all errors since he/she is certain of an errorless mind. Clarity of understanding is certainty (*niscaya*), which is the subject of Chapter Ten.

The fifth and last in the series is, *". . .they realize ultimate nirvana,"* and *". . .have fully awakened . . . ."* This refers of course to bodhi and the highest level of prajna (*adhiprajna*), which is described in Chapter Eleven.

The fourth and fifth prajnas arise from the three root prajnas when developed in order. According to these clues and others within the Heart Sutra we are furnished with a definite and distinct way of development culminating in awakening. These five prajnas are not separate qualities of wisdom, but are meant to indicate the stages of the blossoming of prajna into full awakening. As we will discover further on in this investigation, these five prajnas also accord perfectly with the obvious progression of the Heart Sutra mantra:

gate = srutamayiprajna
gate = cintamayiprajna
paragate = bhavanamayiprajna
parasamgate = niscayamayiprajna
bodhi = adhiprajna

According to the Sutra, the same progression is exactly how awakening comes about.

Studying (sruti) the elements and parts of the text of the Heart Sutra means becoming familiar with terminology and the ideas presented therein. This is the preliminary prerequisite to further and deeper study and expanded analysis of these ideas that entails a thoughtful reflection (cinta). Once the srutamayiprajna arises, it supports the arising of cintamayiprajna. Study is a fairly undeveloped stage but further and deeper reflection does develop through studious enquiry. The Heart Sutra treats study and thoughtful reflection similarly as *gate, gate* – the second *gate* indicating a more thorough progression of the same idea.

Study is the necessary preliminary to the arising of insight (*vipasyana*). This is the format for practice of meditation (bhavana) according to the Heart Sutra. Training (cinta) is the necessary preliminary for gaining confidence and understanding in preparation for meditation by which certainty of the deep truth of emptiness comes about. Training is a deeper level of study, thoughtful reflection. Practice is the practice of meditation through which the first two root prajnas come to fruition. When meditation is successful, the three root prajnas have blossomed and give rise to further perfection of wisdom. Certainty (niscayamayiprajna) then arises and stability in concentration and realization arises with it through persistently advancing through the first three root prajnas. A contemplative practitioner must develop certainty of the truth of emptiness. Simply by understanding the method of the Heart Sutra we can easily become confident of a direct and certain awakening. Fullness (adhiprajna) is the heightened or complete aspect of prajna-wisdom and, in its fullness of holistic apperceptive wisdom, equates with bodhi. This is the culmination of the blossoming of prajna into bodhi and thus, *". . .fully awakening into unsurpassed complete enlightenment through relying on the Profound Perfection of Wisdom."*

This is the explanation of the introductory poem regarding the structure and method of the Heart Sutra that begins our study.

CHAPTER 2

THE TITLE:

ARYA BHAGAVATI PRAJNAPARAMITAHRIDAYASUTRA

This is the full title of the Heart Sutra. Looking at its component parts, *Arya* means "saintly" or "holy", a noble one who has attained, is accomplished or is liberated.

Bhagavati is the key to the structure and method of the Heart Sutra text, and especially the abstract meaning of its mantra.

Prajnaparamitahridayasutra means "Sutra on the Heart of the Transcendent Perfection of Wisdom."

To explore these aspects it is appropriate to begin with the following quote from the sutra:

> *"All the Buddhas of the three times have fully awakened into unsurpassed complete enlightenment through relying on the Profound Perfection of Wisdom."*

This line in the Sutra tells us that all buddhas are born into bodhi from the matrix womb of the Mother (Bhagavati) who herself is prajna. *The One Hundred Thousand Line Sutra on Perfect Wisdom* explains, in the Buddha's words, that, just like a woman with many children is well looked after by them and protected by them because they know she is their mother and has taught them how to live in the world, in the same way the Tathagatas are always mindful of the Perfection of Wisdom. The Tathagatas know very well that prajna is the mother of buddhas, and instructs them in realization of Buddhadharma, which is completed in full enlightenment.

This is the implication of the full title and use therein of the term *Bhagavati*, the feminine grammatical form of *Bhagavat*, the name usually used to refer to the Buddha Sakyamuni. *Bhagavat* means blessed or one who has acquired omniscient wisdom through enlightenment, one who has finished with becoming and perfectly developed himself by doing away with all fears and troubles and by abolishing all defilements like hate, anger, and delusion. All defects have been overcome and such a blessed one is fit to be venerated and relied upon. The term *Bhagavati* in the title is an obvious clue that indicates the proper way to understand the strange grammatical ending of the progressive series of words in the Heart Sutra mantra, *"gate, gate, paragate, parasamgate. . . ."* The verbal ending "te" is the feminine vocative in Sanskrit grammar and has to refer to Bhagavati, Mother Prajnaparamita and her five prajnas just explained in relation to the poem.

The Mahayana iconography of the anthropomorphized Mother Prajnaparamita depicts her sitting in meditation (bhavana) with a book (sruti) and a sword (prajna), the sword of wisdom, double-edged to cut through deceptive conceptual error and the false notion of self. Sometimes there is pictured a vase containing memory (cinta) and the elixir of bodhi (adhiprajna). Her curious smile is not one of humor but one of undeniable certainty (niscaya) and definite incontestability concerning knowledge of the truth. Her halo is the saintly awakened wisdom of bodhi.

The *pra* in Prajnaparamita or prajna is an intensifier, while *jna* means knowledge, understanding and wisdom. The Prajnaparamita texts describe prajna as the highest, supreme, unequaled, incomparable, unsurpassed, superior wisdom. Prajna-wisdom reveals error and unreality and is necessary for the realization of nirvana. Prajna is correct and thorough discrimination, and intense (pra) and profound knowledge (jna) pertaining to three levels of knowing, mundane knowledge, supramundane knowledge, and unsurpassed knowledge.

Mundane knowledge is polluted or wrong knowledge, primal ignorance, getting the real confused with what is unreal. This kind of knowledge usually refers to the Four Perverted Wrong Views explained in Mahayana Buddhism as perversions of perception: thinking that what is actually impermanent is permanent; that what is really a mode of suffering is not so; deeming something lovely when it really is not so; and presuming there is a self when there is really no self.

Supramundane knowledge is knowledge that arises in *sravakas* and *pratyekabhuddas*: knowledge of impermanence, of suffering, of selflessness, and that nirvana is peace. A sravaka is a disciple or student, a hearer of the dharma teachings. A pratyekabuddha is an undeclared enlightened one.

In the foundational doctrine of the Hinayana the awakening experience is described as being any of four basic degrees:

> 1. Stream-enterer, in which the stream or path to nirvana is entered which transcends the self-view, uncertainty, and clinging to practices and habits. The Stream-enterer will be reborn seven times more at most.

2. Once-returner, which is a very substantial overcoming of greed, anger, and delusion. The Once-returner gets reborn only once more.

3. Non-returner, in which sense passions and associated irritations are done away with. The Non-returner goes to the pure abodes or higher heavens and attains nirvana, never again to be reborn in this kind of world.

4. Arhat, which transcends all passion for form and formlessness, self-conceit, restlessness, and ignorance. An Arhat is liberated from the rebirth cycle completely.

5. Pratyekabuddha, which is yet another degree of awakening; one who is privately awakened by understanding the Four Noble Truths but does not teach the path to others.

The third kind of knowledge is called *unsurpassed knowledge*. It is the knowledge of Tathagatas or Buddhas, those who to thusness (tathata) have gone (gata). This is holistic knowledge based on emptiness, that all persons and all phenomena whatsoever are selfless, signless, in a state of wishlessness, and perfect emptiness.

Prajna is the sixth paramita (perfection). The other five paramitas essential to the practice of bodhisattvas are the perfections of giving, morality, patience, vigor, and concentration. Prajna arises as fundamental wisdom only when the veil of ignorance has been overcome and no longer serves as a foundation for errant cognition. Prajna is also analytical wisdom, discriminative excellence, dispassionate clear observation and discernment, knowing things as they really are. Prajna-wisdom is the most crucial of the six perfections because without it the other five cannot be developed. Prajna is the immediate and direct understanding of emptiness and all its implications. Prajna is the ultimate knowing that there is a multiplicity of objects and events but that not a single one of them exists in its own-being since each thing exists only according to prior conditions, dependent on previous conditional factors. So prajna is the knowing of what exists and what does not exist and how things really exist, described profoundly by the Buddhist doctrine of emptiness.

Paramita in the title of the Sutra means perfection, excellence, beyond to consummation. *Param* means beyond and *ita* is that which goes beyond, that which transcends. The Perfection of Wisdom is that final perfect wisdom that directly and correctly discerns all modes and diversities of phenomenal manifestation. It is the buddha-wisdom that overcomes and conquers all conceptual errors and directly and profoundly realizes emptiness. Whosoever else may desire such knowledge and wisdom must study, thoughtfully reflect, and practice meditation.

Hridaya. This word means organism or organized system. The heart is always a functional center of any process or system; without it a system could not function. The system of awakening in Mahayana Buddhism revolves around its heart also, and that is the understanding of emptiness. This word in the title is translated as Heart, meaning center, essence, basis, the core, the pith, the root, the vital part, the essential part, the gist.

Sutra. The meaning of this Sanskrit term is similar to the English word "suture", which is a thread that sews parts together. The suttas and sutras of Buddhism are thus the connected parts of Buddhist doctrine and writings that fit together as to associated meaning and subject matter, way of exposition and explanation. These writings can be short, like the Heart Sutra, or of a middle length, sometimes dozens of pages, or quite long as is found in the Prajnaparamita Sutra in One Hundred Thousand Lines, or the great Avatamsaka and Lotus Sutras which have thousands of pages of scrolls.

This completes the comments on The Title.

CHAPTER 3

THE PROLOGUE

Thus did I hear at one time

In Sanskrit, *evam maya srutam* or *Thus have I heard* or *Thus did I hear* means that someone actually heard the words of that sutra being spoken. This is the common phrase that opens the sutra text, and is consistent in the Pali Suttas and in the Mahayana Sutras. The highest probability of who it was who heard and recorded the discourses originally is Ananda. Some scholars have presumed perhaps someone other than Ananda heard this Heart Sutra and set it to record, and that may be a possibility since usually there is no definite attribution as to whom the exact hearer was. But it was Ananda who was given charge to hear and remember what was said, and to later accurately record the text of each discourse – so the texts themselves proclaim. The Prajnaparamita Sutras record the Buddha as saying,

"Therefore, Ananda, I entrust you with this deep perfection of wisdom. . . . and that if you forget even one verse of it that would be a serious offense. When it has been learned it should be remembered, spoken and studied, analyzed in each letter, syllable, and word. With infinite bestowal I entrust you again with this perfection of wisdom that you may not abandon it or forget even a single word". (paraphrased)

The debate over who actually heard and recorded the Heart Sutra or any other sutra is of little consequence since we still have every word of the texts. When a sutra tells who was present at the discourse it is obvious that all present would have heard the sutra. Although this sutra says that there was *a great gathering of monks and a great gathering of bodisattvas* present, only Ananda had been entrusted with the task of preserving the teaching. In the context of what the Heart Sutra offers, the name of the hearer-recorder is insignificant and there is no reason why it should not be Ananda as in so many other instances.

. . .at one time . . . .

This refers simply to the very instance and occasion when the words of the sutra were spoken and heard.

> *The Conqueror was sitting on Vulture Mountain in Rajagriha with a great gathering of monks and a great gathering of bodhisattvas.*

Conqueror is a name given to the Buddha because he has conquered all ills and suffering, all mental disturbances, all defilements. A conqueror has completely overcome unwholesome mental factors such as delusion, wrong views, greed, hatred, conceit, worry, envy, anger, and many others. He also has the ability to conquer ignorance in the errant minds of others who can learn to reason and see truth.

> *. . .was sitting on Vulture Mountain in Rajagriha . . . .*

This mountain was so named because at its top was, and still is, a huge rock that resembles the profile of a vulture. It is found in Rajagriha in India.

> *. . .with a great gathering of monks and a*
> *great gathering of bodhisattvas.*

In many of the sutras such gatherings were described as huge, numbering thousands of monks and nuns, hundreds of thousands and millions of bodhisattvas, buddhas from billions of world systems, countless devas and innumerable other beings from various planes and dimensions of existence. The descriptions of these gatherings is fantastic and beautiful, promoting the transcendence of limited and constricted mental fabrications and suggesting a gathering of cosmic proportions instead of a small meeting on a mountain top.

In stating that this particular gathering was attended specifically by monks and bodhisattvas, there is indication that the message being given was suitable for both groups. In Buddhism a monk (*bhikshu*) is one who has taken up the official training precepts. For a monk there are five precepts and a bodhisattva usually has ten. A *bodhisattva* is an enlightenment being. The term *bodhi* means enlightenment. *Sattva* means a being with a high or great intention to achieve, a being who is concerned with nirvana for all beings. The sutras define many different levels and varieties of bodhisattvas according to which stages of the path

(*bhumi*) they have attained. The Prajnaparamita
Sutras persistently suggest that one should become
a bodhisattva filled with effort to help all sentient
beings attain enlightenment while engaging in and
promoting compassion throughout all existence.
This bodhisattva aspect is the essential difference
between the Mahayana and the non-Mahayana
schools of Buddhism. Paradoxically these sutras
also stress that there is actually no such thing as a
bhikshu or a bodhisattva, a person or a self. The
solution to this paradox is the understanding of the
deep meaning of sunyata, emptiness. The result of
understanding ensures the right behavior and
activities of a bodhisattva, who knows how to
maintain a balance between *samsara* and nirvana,
between the relative and the absolute, this balance
being the Buddhist Middle Way – detached from
both extremes while realizing the reality of both.

> *At that time the Conqueror was absorbed in*
> *a samadhi on the enumeration of*
> *phenomena called "perception of the*
> *profound."*

The phrase *At that time* denotes the same
occasion of the gathering on Vulture Mountain.
. . .*the Conqueror was absorbed in a samadhi. . . .*
speaks to the fact that the Buddha had entered into

35

a highly concentrated state of mental focus and remained unwavering in it. *Absorbed* means absorption, or a non-distracted applied thought with vigilantly sustained focus. Samadhi is the resultant state of consciousness that occurs when a contemplative is purposefully and intently stabilized in focus upon one thing. When buddhas enter into samadhi all those nearby are also greatly effected in their consciousness, and their understanding is heightened through this association.

> . . .*on the enumeration of phenomena called*
> *"perception of the profound "*.

In the Abhidamma Pitaka, the Pali scriptures which describe in minute detail the Buddhist philosophical psychology, the first of seven books of this "third basket" (pitaka) set of teachings is named the *Dhammasanghani*. The meaning of the title of this first book means "Enumeration of Phenomena". It lists the categories of the elements of existence, states of consciousness, types of different material phenomena, an explanation of all terms used in the sutta (sutra) and Abhidamma (Abhidharma) texts, and condensed explanations of the Abhidhamma system. In this context a phenomenon (dhamma/dharma) is that which is really existent, as well as any object of perception. Since Sariputra plays a crucial part in the Heart Sutra, and the fact that he was the Buddha's Abhidhamma expert, gives a clue as to why this Sutra records that Avalokitesvara explains the Perfection of Wisdom to Sariputra. Sariputra was the greatest protagonist of the wisdom of the Abhidhamma in Buddha's time, and he was a bit perplexed at Prajnaparamita doctrines and its deeper revelation of emptiness.

. . ."*perception of the profound* ".

Something that can only be understood with difficulty is profound, and its perception is that which understands something profoundly, that is, prajna-wisdom.   What is inferred here is the understanding of the meaning of emptiness. The Buddha simultaneously perceives all phenomena as empty in his samadhi and this *"perception of the profound"* indicates the capability of perceiving directly and simultaneously all the categories of phenomena. Those who are as yet unaccomplished cannot do this.   And here this sort of perception refers to the omniscient perception of mahasattva bodhisattvas and buddhas.

A mahasattva, or great being, is one with very great (*maha*) intention or mind of aspiration to achieve the highest, as a distinct quality which other bodhisattvas might not as yet possess, having not reached the higher bhumis, the higher stages of spiritual development.

> *Also at that time, the Bodhisattva, the Mahasattva Avalokitesvara was contemplating the deep meaning of the Profound Perfection of Wisdom and he saw that the five skandhas were all empty of inherent existence.*

Avalokitesvara. The name means "one who is highly capable of great perception and compassionate conduct to those below." The Bodhisattva, Mahasattva Avalokitesvara is here on the tenth and highest bhumi, and his capability is to dispel the suffering of others below this stage by teaching and removing ignorance, ignorance being the first cause of the twelve steps of interdependent origination leading always to suffering and rebirth. This Mahasattva's compassion is directed efficiently to help remove obstructions and errors and to rend the net of delusion.

> *. . .was contemplating the deep meaning of the Profound Perfection of Wisdom . . . .*

When studying and thoughtfully reflecting upon specific subjects with intensity of focus, this practice is called *contemplation*. The Prajnaparamita has *deep meaning* concerning emptiness. Indeed, the whole of the Buddha's work was explaining the deep meaning surrounding the fact of emptiness and the effects of ignorance regarding the truth of the beginning of suffering.

> *. . .and he saw that the five skandhas were all empty of inherent existence.*

When the Sutra says that Avalokitesvara *saw*, it means that he correctly perceived and understood. The five *skandhas* (the constituents that make up conscious personhood, or presumed individuality) are form (*rupa*), feeling (*vedana*), perception (*samjna*), mental formations (*samskara*), and consciousness (*vijnana*). These skandhas, and all phenomena whatsoever, are all empty (*sunya*) of inherent existence, which doesn't mean they don't exist, but does mean they don't exist absolutely. The skandhas, as well as all other objective phenomena do not have ultimacy; they do not exist exclusively as themselves because they arise according to associated conditions that are inclusive of their existence.

Inherent existence connotes something that exists on its own, comes from itself and is no other, but there is no object, no thing, no person, and no set of skandhas (that are taken to be a person) which can self-exist simply because all that can be perceived arises from some set of previous other conditions. Even the previous other conditions arise from their previous other conditions, ad infinitum, and these are not inherently existent either. As such, all things are temporary appearances, but because they are perceived through conceptual delusion they are mistaken for absolute entities, essential realities unto themselves. When emptiness is applied to the errors of perception then pure understanding can arise. This is the function of prajna. When Avalokitesvara *saw* that the five skandhas were all empty of inherent existence, he understood and comprehended correctly the teaching of *anatman*, no-self. The notion of a self based on a collection of skandhas is a suffering-ridden errant notion. In the shorter version of the Heart Sutra there is added here a phrase,

> . . .*thus he overcame all ills and suffering.*

This phrase is a proclamation that the ego-notion, identification with the skandhas, is a root of the origin of suffering. In Buddhism, two of the most difficult subjects to understand correctly are *anatman* (selflessness of person) and *sunyata* (emptiness of phenomena). Primarily they are both the same doctrine. The apparent difference lies in the fact that anatman refers only to the selflessness of a merely conceptually designated person. The fact that a "person" exists only as an errant conceptual designation based on the dependently functioning skandhas is part of the *"perception of the profound"*, and as few ever perceive this truth in its fullness, it is therefore called *profound*.

This completes the comments on The Prologue.

CHAPTER 4

THE QUESTION
AND THE ANSWER

Then, by the power of the Buddha, the Venerable Sariputra said this to the Bodhisattva, the Mahasattva Avalokitesvara, "How should those of good lineage train who wish to practice the Profound Perfection of Wisdom?"

This is a question, a question of great import. It concerns the way of training, and then practice, both of which are based on a development and intensification of understanding of emptiness.

Then, by the power of the Buddha . . . .

What might this strange power be? This power is an empowerment projected by the Buddha so that the teaching may be received and understood by others correctly. Buddhas have various psychic and other powers (*siddhis*) and when they exert them

43

in a certain way those who are nearby are enabled to sense and perceive things that are usually beyond the range of normal senses. When the psychic power is withdrawn, the extended range of sense or understanding diminishes again, but there is a residue of impressions that remain, and the understanding eventually becomes replete and matures into fullness.

> *. . .the Venerable Sariputra . . . .*

When someone has accomplished a stage of the path, or exhibits other reasons to be venerated, respected, or esteemed for noble deeds, that person is sometimes given the title *Venerable.* Sariputra was qualified in many ways to be so regarded.

> *. . . said this to the Bodhisattva, the Mahasattva Avalokitesvara . . . .*

Since both Sariputra and Avalokitesvara were recipients of the Buddha's extended psychic powers, the conversation that is about to begin in depth was, perhaps, spoken for those also nearby who may not have developed such a high level of openness and receptivity as the two named protagonists. Also there was a need to transmute the ideas of this Perfection of Wisdom into words

44

for the benefit of future travelers of the Mahayana Path.

"How should those of good lineage train . . . ."

Good lineage is a line of descent of practitioners who have been practicing the Buddhadharma in the right way, the skillful way as opposed to unskillful ways, or of other traditions outside of the Buddhadharma. Those who adhere to the Way are considered family, and as there are no bad lineages in Buddhism, this *good lineage* includes all monks, bodhisattvas, buddhas and the lay order who conscientiously regard the Buddhadharma. All Buddhist lineages are good lineages when they have conducted themselves rightly, and in this present time both the Theravada and the Mahayana lineages are *good lineages.* All skillful sanghas (Buddhist communities and organization) are *good lineage. Good lineage* usually denotes those who have taken refuge in the Buddha, the Dharma, and the Sangha, and strive to keep true to the precepts.

". . .train . . . ."

Here is the first mention of training in the Heart Sutra, and the word *train* is used in this Sutra once more, just after the mantra. *Train* is equivalent with the right way to view things, or the correct view, as mentioned in the next sentence of the Sutra where the answer to this present question begins. In this commentary, training is equated with thoughtful reflection, the subject of Chapter Eight.

> ". . .who wish to practice the Profound Perfection of Wisdom?"

This is the question. Sariputra wants to know how to train and practice. The training and practice of Prajnaparamita are activities of thought, speech, and action concerned with learning how to understand the correct view, and in this Heart Sutra the emphasis is that emptiness is the correct view as is next given in the answer to Sariputra's question.

> The Bodhisattva, the Mahasattva Avalokitesvara said to the Venerable Sariputra, "Sariputra, sons and daughters of good lineage who wish to practice the Profound Perfection of Wisdom should view things in this way:"

Here begins the answer to Sariputra's question regarding training and practice, and significant in the mention of *sons and daughters of good lineage*. When the original Buddhist sanghas

46

were organized, the Buddha did not exclude females from discipleship or from possibility of attaining enlightenment. At the time of Buddha this was considered a radical departure from most other traditions of established social structure. The more modern feminist movements were preceded by 2500 years with the Buddha's inclusion of females as equal in the sangha.

" . . .should view things in this way: . . . ."

The *training* is how to view things. The *training* is the necessary preliminary to the *practice,* and in order that practice (bhavana) be performed correctly, the view of the practitioner must be correct and not defiled and delusional in some way. The view, or the way to view things in accord with the perspective of emptiness, is the basis or support of right meditation in order that thought and consequent behavior will be concordant with the Perfection of Wisdom.

The Heart Sutra has thus delineated the three root prajnas within its own text with the keywords *contemplating* (study), *training* (thoughtful reflection), and *practice* (meditation).

"They should correctly view the five skandhas also as empty of inherent existence . . . ."

This sentence tells us what actually is the correct view. It is emptiness of the five skandhas.

". . .the five skandhas . . . ."

These five skandhas are the aggregates of which a living being and personality is composed. Skandha is a Sanskrit term with the meaning of a group, a cluster, aggregates, a combination, an organized assemblage, a composite collection.

Form is the material aggregate and includes all objects involved in sense perception and includes the human body generally. Form can include that which seems outside the body as objective phenomena, and also mental formations produced subjectively internally within mind, mind being also considered the sixth sense.

Feelings pertain to sensation, associated with tactile pressures that are then mentally construed as being pleasurable, painful, or neutral. There is also a mental aspect to feelings, finding expression in emotional responses designated as pleasurable, painful, or neutral. Feeling is a condition necessary for the arising of clinging.

Perceptions refer to all functions of perceptive interpretation in the objective field. The word *conception* is often used in place of or in addition to the idea of *perception* in the sense of not only perceiving the aspects of things felt in some way, but also entering into a mental discussion regarding those aspects.

Mental formations include all types of thought structure, patterns, and qualities of mind that give impetus to action. The Buddha taught that mental formations were karma and that with the arising of these, action occurs, be it by body, speech, or mind.

Consciousness is that awareness that arises from the impressions of sense data via conditions sensed as objects. This skandha might be described as the basic cognitive potential, while the other skandhas provide more specific functions with their definite qualities. Apart from conditions, there is no consciousness, and so it is possible to notate innumerable kinds of consciousness according to innumerable conditions affecting the aggregates of a body-mind complex we usually think of as a person.

It states in the Prologue section that Avalokitesvara *saw that the five skandhas were all empty of inherent existence.* Likewise it is again stressed in his answer to Sariputra that those who seek should also view the skandhas as empty, . . .*empty of inherent existence,* just as he had discovered beforehand.

What is meant by *empty of inherent existence*? The skandhas, being the constituents of the individual psychosomatic equipment that makes up what is usually called the person and the personality, "self", are of two types. The human body is form. The mind is feelings, perceptions, mental formations, and consciousness generally. A group, or a composite collection of factors such as make up the definition of skandhas, cannot be classified as intrinsically a "self" of some sort. They do not constitute a self-entity. A sum of different parts cannot be a self-entity simply because we assume it to be somehow different from its parts. There is no inherent self in the form we label as our body.

A perception is not, nor does it make a personal self, nor do feelings or mental formations or their subsequent willed actions. The perceptions do not constitute selfhood because they are made up of and brought into momentary being by various sense windows and objects, none of which have permanent self-essence within themselves. All phenomenal things, these so-called entities, are susceptible to the same analysis. A cart cannot be considered as having inherent self-cartness because in the absence of its parts it does not exist except as an idea in our consciousness. It is a created agglomeration serving a momentary purpose, but nothing more. Nor do its parts have permanency or self existence; they are merely temporal objects that we create names for according to their specific functions. A wheel is not a cart, and parts which make up the wheel do not make a wheel in their sum except in our mind. The axle is not a cart, nor is any other part a cart. "Cart" is a name given by mind to the collection of parts collectively forming the functional object. Nor does the wood or metal formed and shaped into the making of the axle make an axle. The object, along with each of its parts, is empty of self-nature. Even the parts are made of yet other composite parts, all being empty of self-nature. This pertains to the smallness of microcosms ad infinitum; it also pertains to the largeness of macrocosms ad infinitum. Each and every thing involved in beingness, and in the parts of the being's part-ness, is all *process*, the process we call change and function.

Tree, which provides wood, is a composite of many intricate parts, most of which we are blissfully unaware, and in its more apparent being we see it as roots, leaves, twigs, branches, trunk, bark, cones, seed pods, and so on, all together in some varied formations. Collectively all parts are similar, yet individually they are dissimilar. But there is no eternal and unchanging essence called tree, or tree in any of its manifest varied forms and names. All are empty of permanent entity. It, like all things, is simply a process in action, the sum of its functioning parts, destined because of its arising to also be in a state of change which culminates in its ceasing to be, wherein its various component parts also move through their own states of change, all following the same dharma as outlined in the laws governing interdependent origination as it pertains to all objects in all conditions. These so-called entities are all identical in fact, whether functioning on a macro level or on a micro level, from cosmic expanse to the tiniest atomic impulse. REALITY is emptiness, and the ultimate boundaries into which our consciousness can function leaves us with something indefinable that we feel we have to define, giving that very state a form and name that is in itself ultimately emptiness of enduring beingness.

This does not mean that things do not exist; it only means they don't exist absolutely. Usually we perceive things wrongly, conceptually designating or naming things. Doing so does not make them real self-entities. But because of communication necessities, we do so and begin to take our societal mind-creations seriously as being real and enduring parts of "our" existence. Because our bodily skandhas function in the way they do, and because the basic storehouse consciousness carries the karmic seeds responsible for our habits and impulses toward action, we maintain our chronic internal dialogues and delusional attitudes, especially regarding a supposed internal self somewhere in the body. It is this supposed self that we usually think is directing experiences, directing the body, and generally calling the shots throughout each day. But, just like all else, all sentient beings in whatever form and with whatever degree of consciousness, according to appropriate conditions available, will follow the laws governing its beingness, and those aspects which make up its aggregational "birth" will react accordingly, following the process of interdependent origination without cease, moving through the process of change flawlessly. If we can understand how the process works, we can cut the knot of our own helpless entanglement in it.

In Mahayana Buddhism there are posited a total of nine aspects of consciousness. Familiarity with these will help in understanding the process of perception and knowing. These nine are:

The five sense consciousnesses;
The sixth is *manovijnana*;
The seventh is *klistomanas*;
The eighth is *alayavijnana*;
The ninth is the *amalavijnana*.

The five sense consciousnesses are awareness of external sense data through the five organs of sense: eyes, ears, nose, tongue, and body. Manovijnana is considered as a sixth sense co-ordinating the observations of the five senses. Manovijnana is the intellect, the thought process that judges by comparing and distinguishing the various sense data. The seventh, klistomanas, is enthralled with clinging to the idea of separate self, the notion of ego, the mental identification with the skandhas. The klistomanas is "defiled" because it habitually discriminates between "self" and "other" and deposits these karmic seeds (*bija*) in the storehouse consciousness, the eighth. The ninth is the amalavijnana that has been cleansed of all the polluted or unwholesome seed impressions.

The klistomanas creates an illusion of an ego-identity, a self, where there is only the skandhas and psychological phenomena. Klistomanas has been called "the defiled mind" and for good reason. It is the source of errant dualistic perceptions and dichotomies, the splitting of a oneness of changing flux into two or more supposed parts without realizing the real non-separateness, emptiness, according to the laws of interdependent origination. Klistomanas is the intermediary between the six senses and the storehouse consciousness. In order to repair the dysfunctional thought process it is necessary to eliminate the false assumptions and dichotomizing discriminations to which it is habituated. Insights gained through study, thoughtful reflection and meditation heal the illness of the klistomanas and it then ceases to deliver polluted seed impressions to the storehouse consciousness. The storehouse consciousness then collects no additional unwholesome seed impressions and those seeds already formed within begin to wither away due to lack of sustenant energy given to them by errant thought. When the storehouse is without the seeds of delusion it is called amalavijnana. This is the gist of the process, of which more is given in the chapters on meditation and the mantra.

Remember, all "things" arise dependent on previously arisen conditional states. Reality is the eternal absence of presumption of self-existing things. We experience reality as-it-is *not* because of a dysfunctional imaginative process, but only through a process of discriminative acuity, of shedding delusion and letting go of clinging, ego-based attitudes and habitual misperception as explained and presented by Avalokitesvara in this sutra gem. All things, including our presumed "self", are empty.

This completes the comments on The Question and the Answer.

CHAPTER 5

THE NEGATIONS

"O, Sariputra, form is none other than emptiness and emptiness is none other than form. Form is emptiness and emptiness is form."

The Negations section of the Heart Sutra is a series of clarifying statements that nullify conceptual inferences regarding the real or separate existence of any object whatsoever, whether of material form or of mental pattern. The tactic of negation is a process of deconstructing conceptual errors. A further section of the Sutra reminds us that bodhisattvas passing beyond all errors realize ultimate nirvana. That realization is the result of the transcendence of obstructive fabricated mental structures which the Heart Sutra and other Prajnaparamita Sutras encourage. Having dedicated himself to the path of progress of the bodhisattva of the great Middle Way of the Buddhadharma, a practitioner meets with great texts and great teachers, helpers along the Way. The knowledge and instruction in the Heart Sutra promotes quick and effective progress through a method whereby mental effluents and obscuring structures are subtracted rather than using a method of adding vast sums of knowledge.

There are many and various cognitive obstructions to progress, some so obnoxious as to curtail further advancement or even to set the traveler on the Way into a reversal of direction. The modus operandi of an adept traveler or contemplative, therefore, is to remove or subtract these hindrances by identifying them and recognizing their detrimental effects. There is nothing quite so obstructive as false or wrong views; yet such views can be eliminated through recognition of their falsity. Nothing has to be added; no addition need be pursued. The Prajnaparamita texts teach the art of transcending delusion by subtracting conceptual error and deconstructing errant mental structures.

A Sanskrit word that pertains to such a deconstruction process is *apoha*, or "what something is not". Here the method of the Negations section puts an inferential emphasis on the uniqueness of whatever is being regarded; what something really is is clearly realized by *apoha*, an analysis of what it is not, thereby putting it in the correct conceptual context of its interdependency within the relativity of existence. Any thing, event, or object is actually a non-separate, functional aspect of the totality of relativity – plus the cognition of it. The correct cognition of anything is an application of attention that can intercept the habitual flow of the distracted mind in its incessant deluded thinking. More than a restructuring of the mind by addition of more complexity, the Prajnaparamita dialectic is actually a process of deconstructing false views that in their absence, allows the enlightened condition of prajna to function according to the truth of sunyata. This kind of perception is prajna-wisdom.

When Avalokitesvara tells Sariputra that *". . .form is none other than emptiness, and emptiness is none other than form"* he means to eliminate any error of thinking that might suggest that form and emptiness are two different things. Emptiness is only a concept, a potent idea that can negate all other fictitious ideas and formats of thinking. Material form is never different from emptiness because emptiness is just a pure perception of form as it really is, with no conceptual overlay added on by an errant mental function such as attraction or repulsion, preference or prejudice. Neither form nor emptiness can be a separate reality. If form is cognized in any manner other than as empty, or being free from absolute individuality or separateness, then a conceptual overlay, or superimposition, by the fabricating mind, is taking place. This is the distinguishing trait of delusion, seeing something askew, seeing something as other than it really is.

Emptiness is a deconstruction device to be used to purify an errant cognitive process. The right way to know form is to know it as empty of inherent existence. Form is emptiness because emptiness negates form as existent unto itself. If emptiness and form were different entities, then it would be possible to assert their realities as separate from one another. The real way form exists is in emptiness of inherent existence. The only way emptiness exists is because it is the reality of form. They cannot be a duality opposed to each other, nor can they be separate from one another. They both are interdependent, therefore non-different.

"Form is emptiness and emptiness is form."

Here is the natural positive conclusion that arises when the conceptual duality of form and emptiness has been negated.

"The same is true for feelings, perceptions, mental formations, and consciousness."

60

The true meaning of emptiness and form as non-dual wisdom has just been spoken by Avalokitesvara and now he includes the other four skandhas as partaking of the same truth. All the skandhas are emptiness and emptiness is all the skandhas.

> *"Sariputra, all phenomena are characteristically empty, not created nor destroyed, neither tainted nor pure, without increase or decrease."*

The Heart Sutra extends the purview of emptiness to include all phenomena. Emptiness is their real characteristic, their distinctive markless mark. Emptiness is not just another conceptual overlay imposed on an object of perception, and because of this it is not a real mark or a real characteristic as imputed by the mind. Empty is how things really are, how things really exist in the constantly evolving state of change.

> *". . .not created nor destroyed . . . ."*

Any objective phenomena, coarse or subtle, of materiality or of mentality, is empty of its own selfness and completely interdependent in its relational interplay with all else in existence.

Something can be "created" only when it previously has no existence whatsoever, but there is no such thing because whatever exists arises into existence from prior conditionality.

Conditionality must be considered empty of its own inherent existence since it cannot exist apart from its impermanency. There is absolutely no phenomenon that has definite boundaries or limits of self-existence, separate, originating from its own essential basis, or existing as an absolutely singular, one-only entity. This is why a particular phenomenon, even the totality of phenomena, cannot be created or destroyed. Conditions, which *things* really are, emerge from previous sets of conditions and those conditions merge into another status which we give a name to conceptually, and then habitually perceive (erroneously) as being a singular phenomenon.

". . .neither tainted nor pure . . . ."

The terms *tainted* and *pure* are conceptual imputations, the superimposition of mental factors projected onto objects of perception. These mental factors have nothing to do with the objects as they really are.

". . .without increase or decrease."

These are the same kinds of conceptual distortions, notions that are applied to an object that is assumed to exist separately as itself only, instead of how it really exists, the flux of conditions continually changing. In the absence of such mistaken assumptions, clarity is experienced and notions such as *tainted*, *pure*, *increase* and *decrease* are known as they really are, as only partial descriptions, mental situations not to be confused with the real "empty" state of things.

> *"Therefore, Sariputra, in emptiness there are no forms, no feelings, no perceptions, no mental formations, no consciousness."*

When a conclusion follows a premise that sets forth an explanation, it is indicated by the word "therefore", which here is intended to further extend the instruction on emptiness by means of negation. Again, Sariputra is reminded that all the five skandhas are empty of inherent existence.

> *". . .no eyes, no ears, no nose, no tongue, no body, no mind;"*

These are the six sense media, or sense organs.

"no form, no sound, no odor, no taste, no touch, no object of mind."

These are the six sense objects of the six sense organs and their detectable phenomena. The six sense media and the six sense objects taken together are called the twelve sense bases.

"There is no realm of eyes and so forth, up to and including no mind consciousness."

This statement refers to the six classes of consciousness that are cognitions related to the six sense organs and their six objects of contact. The cognitions, along with the six sense organs and their six contact objects, are classified as being eighteen elements. These are the essential dynamics of consciousness incident in the course of conscious awareness and coincident with other factors like sensitivity, external conditions, light, attention, duration, and a multiplicity of accumulated mental factors and qualities that can misconstrue and distort. Keeping this in mind, the meaning of the above quoted statement is that these eighteen elements are nothing more than names and descriptions of partialities; of fractions of interdependent and interrelated processes we term "condition(s)", temporary aspects of cognitive cycles, none of which have their own inherent existence. There is no state of permanent "eye-ness" out of which eye arises full blown, as from the mind of Zeus. There is no state of permanent "anything-ness" out of which any "thing" arises full blown from its own inherent selfness.

". . .and so forth, up to and including . . . ."

This is a way of declaring the more detailed formula previously given in the Sutra in a more abbreviated way.

The 18 Elements of Consciousness

form	sound	odor	taste	sensation	mental object
eyes	ears	nose	tongue	body	mind
eye c.	ear c.	nose c.	tongue c.	body c.	mind c.

"There is no ignorance and no extinction of ignorance and so forth, up to and including no ageing and no death and also no extinction of ageing and death."

This sentence is another radical negation, this time of the important Buddhist doctrine of interdependent origination. Just prior to his enlightenment in the third watch of the night, the Buddha comprehensively considered the twelve links of interdependent origination. The twelve links,

65

correctly and fully comprehended, are a necessary foundation for understanding the reality of emptiness. This formula shows that whatever comes about emerges from a prior condition, and so, being dependent on previous factors, must necessarily be empty of essential selfness. These twelve links are:

> **1**. Ignorance: That which is defined as not knowing the Four Noble Truths of suffering, origin of suffering, cessation of suffering, and the path leading to the cessation of suffering.
>
> **2**. Fabrications: These are the active karmic volitional formations, bodily, verbal, and mental.
>
> **3**. Consciousness: The six classes of consciousness arising from sense contact, eye contact, ear contact, etc.
>
> **4**. Name and Form: Regarding name, there is feeling, perception, intention, contact, and attention. Regarding form there are the four great elements of earth, water, fire, and air.
>
> **5**. Six Sense Organs: The organs of eye, ear, nose, tongue, body, and mind.
>
> **6**. Contact: The six contact classifications arising through eye, ear, nose, etc.
>
> **7**. Feeling: The cognitive awareness of pleasure, of pain, of neither pleasure nor

pain, born in the six classes according to the six sense contacts.

8. Craving: The desire (attachment) born of feelings arising from the pleasurable contacts of the six sense media.

9. Clinging-sustenance: Shows itself in four aspects: clinging to sensuality, to view, to precept and practice, and to the doctrine of "self".

10. Becoming: Becoming pertains to sensual becoming, form becoming, and formless becoming.

11. Birth: This process involves the interdependent origination involving the mental conditions conducive to rebirth, descent, coming to be, the appearance of the aggregates, acquisition of sense organs, etc.

12. Aging and Death: The result of rebirth, decrepitude, brokenness, graying, wrinkling, decline, weakening of faculties, the decreasing of strengths, the breaking up, passing away, disappearing, – the dying process, etc.

The way it is is that each thing or event is a unique phenomenon, a structure of infinite conditionality. Each condition therein is also a unique phenomenon. The uniqueness of each phenomenon is so only relative to the rest of conditionality; it is the totality of the flux which makes relativity possible. It has been said that the understanding of interdependent origination is the key to understanding emptiness, which in turn is the key to enlightenment. Why then is this doctrine of interdependent origination also negated in the Heart Sutra?

Actually the Sutra does not really negate the fact of interdependent origination, it merely states that its twelve components are not self-existing either. What the Sutra negates is the perception that these components arise and exist independently, of themselves. But this cannot be so because conditionality itself is a set of conditions, just as is every condition within conditionality.

". . .no extinction . . . ."

Here is another negation of what Buddhism presents as foundational doctrines. Avalokitesvara is not saying that these doctrines do not exist, but how they exist is that they are not separate or self-existing classes and elements of nature, but can exist only as conceptual aspects of a totality. Avalokitesvara's radical statements in the Heart Sutra are not an attack on the established profound truths of Buddhism, but a defense of the fact that the understanding of emptiness through prajna-wisdom must be applied throughout all the doctrinal bases. The extinction of ignorance and of ageing and death means there can be *no extinction* of something that has no real self-existence. These, like all else, will always arise again and again as conditions become fertile for another repetitive round; yet the components of the repetitions are selfless, the repetitions are selfless, and all that appears to originate is selfless. Process IS, but it is also selfless.

The same application of emptiness is valid here concerning the Four Noble Truths, which are:

The Noble Truth
of Suffering

The Noble Truth
of the Origin of Suffering

The Noble Truth
of the Cessation of Suffering

The Noble Truth of the Path
Leading to the Cessation of Suffering

The last Truth consists of Right View, Right Thought, Right Speech, Right Action, Right Livelihood, Right Effort, Right Mindfulness, and Right Concentration.

Within this list there are no pills, no right foods, no right monies, no right homes and gardens, no right education, no right religious denomination, no right upbringing or social standard. There is only unattached being, like a newly created pot on a wheel is satisfied with being that which it is, and nothing more. It is said,

> *"There is no wisdom and no attainment with nothing to attain."*

And even this statement is applicable. These terms are only conceptual descriptions of ideas that should not be viewed as something other than what they really are. The fundamental disciplines of Buddhism culminate in knowing what exists and what does not exist, which is the eradication of delusion – which is itself also subject to this negation. All is flux, conditional change, with no separate or entirely individual thing undergoing the changes. There are only momentary mistakenly perceived impressions of unchanging individuality in this soup of swirling currents, in this tightly interwoven textual fabric of many hues. Here *wisdom* refers to prajna and *attainment* refers to nirvana. It is not that prajna and nirvana do not exist at all; it is that neither have their own substantial independent existence. They are simply states of being, just another condition arising within the conditional, and their truth as a concept is no more substantial than is "tree" or "forest".

The Heart Sutra utilizes a negative dialectic because real apperceptive knowing must transcend the limited terms of discriminative thinking and the habitual structures of perception that are incomplete and limited when using conventionalities of language that can transmit counterfeit thought-forms, errant modes of imperfect expression.

Since the first expression in negative terms that emptiness and form are non-distinct, Avalokitesvara has told Sariputra that basically nothing exists as it is commonly perceived to exist – nothing whatsoever; even the hallowed doctrines of Buddhism do not exist autonomously, and there is nothing that can be known correctly through conceptual or verbal designations. The communication of sunyata through the device of negation is a potent and effective approach that can lead to direct immediate experience. What things really are cannot be affected by any terminological description of them; they are simply and only what they are. But discriminative error makes for delusion. Emptiness does not imply non-existence or nihilism. Emptiness is only a device that puts to rest all wrong distractions and distinctions and allows passage *beyond all errors.*

> *"Therefore, Sariputra, because bodhisattvas have nothing to attain they rely on abiding in the Profound Perfection of Wisdom without mental hindrances."*

A further stage in the summation of what was said before, Avalokitesvara here mentions that *". . .bodhisattvas have nothing to attain . . . ."* The Perfection of Wisdom Sutras explain in manifold ways that nothing can really be attained or achieved because any perceivable object or goal is merely a mentally or verbally designated idea. A bodhisattva has nothing to attain because "bodhisattva" too is a mental and verbal designation, a name applied to a set of conditions as if that bodhisattva were an extant self arising in independent separate completeness. An individual perceiving itself as a bodhisattva self, or for that matter any other type of self-being, is delusional perception, creating an own-self using the same errant thinking methods arising from fundamental ignorance.

Similarly, it is an error to apprehend any thing as being impermanent. Buddhadharma points out that all is impermanent, arising and abiding for a time, yet naturally and eventually dissolving away, changing into something else. But if there is no real self-being of anything, anywhere, at any time, then there actually can be no thing, and no correct description of it. So there can be no thing to describe as being impermanent because there is no permanent self-thing. In the deeper vision of emptiness, so-called "things" or dharmas, are known to be a flux of changing events, or a simple changing-ness. But there is really no independent singular thing that undergoes a change. Therefore, as Avalokitesvara has said, "there is nothing to attain." *Attainment*, as an event that someone or something arrives at, cannot really be so, and so has to be negated and known as a corrupt conceptualization. Ultimate attainment then is this: In the absence of such wrong-apprehension the correct view will BE. The correct being of pot-ness is simply the attainment of the momentary state of being a pot without any other amendments of any sort whatsoever, with correct discrimination of exactly what pot and pot-ness really are.

The gist of the Heart Sutra is that the whole motivation to *attain* what is desired, even if that should be a liberation or an enlightenment, is a futile gesture based on partial and errant observation and thinking. To simply cease thinking in the wrong way, or unskillfully, is to simultaneously cease the entanglements, transcend the hindrances and obstructions, vacate the wrong motivations, wrong behaviors, and wrong views. Immediately bodhi is experienced as perfect awareness, the awareness that has been available at all times anyway, like the shadow always moving by our side. But because of such a density of obstructed perceptive qualities this presence is not readily perceived. If one can cease errant apprehensions, subtract them and see without errant discrimination, that is what is necessary. Nothing has to be attained. Thus there is "*no attainment*". It might be said that one has then obtained or attained an "absence" of delusion, which is a definition of bodhi and of nirvana, but an "absence" cannot be an attainment because an absence is a void of anything existing therein. Absence is discerned as a condition that has no conditions, a double negative, an unconditional non-condition, the same as the double negative "*no non-attainment*". This is a dialectic verbal method that negates something that could never be in any case, so the truth is revealed.

> ". . .they rely on abiding in the Profound
> Perfection of Wisdom without mental
> hindrances."

The primary hindrance alluded to here is the hindrance of wrong view, of not understanding emptiness and self. The five hindrances (*nivarana*) in Buddhist terminology are usually sense desire, ill will, sloth and torpor, restlessness and worry, and doubt. In the absence of hindrances, there is no fear because a bodhisattva is not shaken by the anxiety of losing something or of not attaining something because his discrimination is no longer faulty; it is founded in emptiness. There is no thing that has an exclusively self-subsistent nature, so whatever does not absolutely exist cannot be lost, or attained. There can be then no fear of loss, no fear of non-attainment. Fear arises only out of the apprehension that something undesirable may happen or that something desirable may not happen. But what does not exist cannot either be lost or retained. When a totalistic perspective is known as truth, then there can be no fear, no foreboding, no dread, no despair, because all is recognized as it really is, as selfless. Truth is the state of non-created being. Truth sets one free. It is the ego-motivated restless mind, creating stress, distraction, diversion, that inseminates rebirth in any form. Ignorance creates images of self and a busy mind never sees the attendant shadow-truth that is always part and parcel of the momentary process. Therefore, it is said that abiding in the Profound Perfection of Wisdom *without mental hindrances*, the bodhisattvas *are without fear*. And the reality of this understanding is the realization of relativity within wholeness and wholeness within relativity.

> *"Having passed completely beyond all errors they realize ultimate nirvana."*

Errors are wrong beliefs, incorrect understanding of the nature of something. There are sixty-two diverse kinds of wrong beliefs delineated in the Pali Suttas and the Mahayana Sutras. An error of perception, a misunderstanding, creates a mental condition where one believes something to be true when it is not, or something to be not true when it is. Such mental errors are the root of transgressions in all behavioral contexts be they manners, morals, or ethics. Nirvana is the fact of experience only when all errors have been *passed completely beyond*. The situation is bodhi, a state of perfected prajna-wisdom in which there is transcendent understanding, perfection of awareness of emptiness of things and of self, awareness of flux, awareness of reality as that condition of conceptual non-creation. This is seeing truly, without the filtering hindrances and errors. This is *ultimate nirvana*.

> *"All the buddhas of the three times have fully awakened into unsurpassed, complete enlightenment through relying on the Profound Perfection of Wisdom."*

Prajna is the only mother of all buddhas. There is no other mother. *"All the buddhas of the three times"* usually refers to the buddhas of the past who came before Sakyamuni Buddha, the present dispensation of Sakyamuni Buddha, and the future Buddha-to-be, Maitreya.

This completes the comments on The Negations.

CHAPTER 6

THE MANTRA

> *"Therefore, the mantra of the Profound Perfection of Wisdom is the mantra of great knowledge, the unsurpassed mantra. The incomparable mantra, the mantra which thoroughly allays all suffering without fail."*

The original text of the Heart Sutra reads: *mahamantro, maha-vidya mantro, 'nuttara mantro samasamamantrah . . . .* The meaning of the Sanskrit term *mantra* is "mind guardian". The inference is that the mind needs to be guarded or protected because somehow it is off the true course, or is susceptible to corruption or invasion. The meditative use of the Heart Sutra mantra will be detailed later.

> *". . .the great mantra . . . ."*

The Sanskrit word for *great mantra* in the Heart Sutra text is *mahamantro*. Here *great* indicates something exalted, majestic, regal, or royal.

". . .the mantra of great knowledge . . . ."

What kind of knowledge is *great knowledge*? The Sanskrit words are *maha-vidya mantro. Great Knowledge* exceeds both mundane knowledge and supramundane knowledge and refers to unsurpassed knowledge, the knowledge of a Buddha.

". . .the unsurpassed mantra . . . ."

The word *unsurpassed* was used just previously in the Sutra text, *". . .fully awakened into unsurpassed, complete enlightenment . . . ."* and here it has the same connotation. This is the mantra that can lead to bodhi; it is unexcelled, unequaled, and it is matchless. There is no other mantra that can be better for the task.

". . .the incomparable mantra . . . ."

Exceptional, superior, and perfect is this mantra.

". . .the mantra which thoroughly allays all suffering . . . ."

Completely, painstakingly, absolutely, and totally is the meaning of *thoroughly* in this line. *Allay* means to relieve and alleviate, so when

78

suffering is understood, it can go the way of all mental creations; it is gone, really gone, it is allayed. The condition causing the suffering is modified in mind's response, and the negative reactive response is eliminated accordingly.

> ". . .without fail".

These two words are an assurance, a complete guarantee that this mantra will not be found lacking.

> "Because it is not false it is known as true."

Here is the sum total and final statement of all that has been previously given in the Heart Sutra text and represented by the mantra. This line hints once again at *apoha*, the knowing of something as it is by understanding what it is not. The mantra is true because it is certain, definite, and genuine. It is known as true, not merely believed in, by those who learn to use it. Belief is a theory; knowing is experiential and direct.

Exploring the mantra itself, and its meditative aspects, the mantra of the Profound Perfection of Wisdom is stated:

"Tadyatha Om Gate Gate Paragate Parasamgate Bodhi Svaha!"

"Tadyatha . . . ."

The meaning of *Tadyatha* is "it is thus".

". . .om . . . ."

In Buddhism *om* is called the "bejeweled mantra"; it is ornamented with the infinite jewels of Buddhadharma and thus bestows blessings of wisdom. Characteristically it is used as an addition to some Buddhist mantras, becoming a symbol of spiritual knowledge, most specifically knowledge of *emptiness.*

". . .gate . . . ." (pronounced *guh-tay.*)

Gate means "move", "goes", "proceeds forward"; "ga" means "movement"; *"te"* is the feminine vocative ending mentioned previously. Some translators render *gate* as "gone" but "gone" is past tense and grammatically written with a final *"a"*, *gata.* A common title for a buddha is *tathagata,* "one thus gone".

So what is it that moves? The clue is in the title of the Heart Sutra, the word *Bhagavati.* So we know that it is Mother Prajnaparamita who moves or goes, and as she iconographically represents prajna-wisdom, it becomes obvious that it is prajna that moves or goes, *gate.*

The second repeat of the word *gate* is a progressive extension of the first *gate*, giving the meaning of prajna moving further, but in the same manner.

"*. . .paragate . . . .*"

The prefix *para* has the meaning "beyond". *Paragate* means "prajna moves beyond".

"*. . .parasamgate . . . .*"

The Sanskrit preposition *sam* has the meaning of "together", "simultaneous", "joined", something holistically integrated. *Parasamgate* then indicates that "prajna moves beyond integrally". This describes accurately the integration of the arising of srutamayiprajna, cintamayiprajna, bhavanamayiprajna, and niscayamayiprajna, which joined simultaneously together are called adhiprajna (higher understanding), which is the engenderment of bodhi.

"*. . .bodhi . . . .*"

The high wisdom of adhiprajna is holistic wisdom, awakened awareness. It creates the habitual knowing that leads meditatively to the un-thinking state of awareness, the reality state of knowing beyond dependently originated mind-creation, the state of awakened enlightenment, *bodhi.*

". . .*svaha!*"

This is the final exclamation of the Heart Sutra mantra and has the meaning "it is just so." It leaves no doubt as to the validity of this "progression" that takes place. But what exactly is happening as described in this mantra?

There is contained here something of deep meaning. When Prajna moves (*gate*) there is no one who is moving, nobody with his own self-nature going from here to there. Wisdom itself is moving to perfection; consciousness is being purified. The completion of wisdom's purification is personified by tathagatas who ". . .*having passed completely beyond all error . . . .*" are "thus gone". They have traversed the path, they have been there, they have seen it, they have done it, and they have winnowed the grain of its chaff and achieved the goal, moving beyond the realm of effort, having fully digested even the cleansed heads of grain, yet attaining nothing, ". . .*with nothing to attain.*"

Bodhi is the arrival, seeing reality. With this arrival one no longer experiences a movement of wisdom. One IS wisdom. Bodhi is not a place traveled to. Bodhi has not a location. Bodhi is a consciousness event. Purified wisdom is an absence of error, an ultimate achievement of seeing, a state of awareness we call *nirvana.*

The first *gate* indicates the movement engendered through study, through language and its influence on the creative consciousness. It might be said that *gate* is the portal through which one moves in the process of purification, the elimination of negative seeds permeating the storehouse consciousness. The second emphatic *gate* empowers a continuation of the first influential movement, but to a heightened degree of the first movement in awareness. Thoughtful reflections and meditative absorption into the nature of this movement deepen knowledge and realizations first brought into view by study.

Paragate takes the movement of prajna beyond study and analytical reflection into the actual practice of meditation that will give direct experiential understanding, awareness beyond whatever can be known just through reasoning and analysis as enjoyed by the sensually conscious but essentially ignorant state of discrimination. Meditation produces a definitive experience of certainty regarding that previously studied and reflected upon. The deeper the meditative state achieved, the more clear becomes the integration of wisdom. The discriminating mind is relieved of its tasks, and seeing becomes as a mind-mirror experiencing phenomena with no thought beyond the purity of the reflection as reality being as it really is at that moment. It is here that *parasamgate* is. Everything integrates. Aspects are moved beyond. Adhiprajna! Bodhi! It is just SO. *Svaha*! The way it is IS the way it is, and the only way it could be. Therefore, away with dualistic language and its ever-creating confusion. But alas, how can the Sutra or this commentary exist without those words? So, onward, because this too is "just so".

The movement into bodhi is in fact a movement away from perceptive error and wrong understanding. It is a movement without a mover; it is a going without a goer. It is a movement without any designation. There is no place, no time, no goal, no achiever, no traveler; there is only the reality hidden beneath obscuring mental creation awaiting. The present apperceptive awareness is fact, as reality, as pure being, when the superimposed mental factors are left behind, gone beyond. The absence of conceptive error can occur only in the present moment, just as delusion can occur only in the present. So to plan for an awakening in some future is to deny the reality that underlies the present NOW moment, and is fuel for the continuation of rebirth and death in its manifold forms. The importance of rightly understanding sunyata, emptiness, through this process of apoha, knowing what things are by knowing what they are not, is the very trigger mechanism allowing for the errant perceptive function's progressive dwindle culminating in this prajna movement that reaches its apex in the purified and non-discriminating NOW bodhi moment.

> *"Sariputra, Bodhisattva Mahasattvas should train in the Profound Perfection of Wisdom in just this way."*

This way is the way of apperceptive wisdom that is beyond the interference of all residual artifacts of tendencies and proclivities.

This completes the comments on The Mantra.

CHAPTER 7

THE EPILOGUE

Then the Conqueror rose from that samadhi and said to the Bodhisattva, the Mahasattva Avalokitesvara, "Well done, well done, well done, child of good lineage; it is just that way."

The Conqueror is the Buddha Sakyamuni, and his samadhi was mentioned in the prologue as *The enumerations of phenomena called "perception of the profound"*. Three times *"well done"* may seem like wordiness or redundancy, but the Buddha is really applauding Avalokitesvara, *"well done"*, acclaiming the discourse *"well done"*, and sanctioning its message *"well done"*. Three times *"well done"* indicates that the message of the Heart Sutra is sufficient for progress through mundane knowledge, supramundane knowledge, and beyond into completion of unsurpassed knowledge.

". . .it is just that way."

This is near to the same meaning of svaha as found in the mantra. That's the way it is. You hit the nail right on the head.

> ". . .the Profound Perfection of Wisdom should be practiced just as you have taught it."

This is a further sanction and reminder of the deep systematic procedure to be learned from the Heart Sutra.

> "Even the Tathagatas admire this."

That perfected beings esteem and honor such wisdom as has been presented in the Heart Sutra discourse is a profound statement showing the significance and value of the Sutra. All buddhas have gone to the realization of their state using the same course of action. There is a way, and the way is the way of no way.

> The Conqueror, having thus spoken, the Venerable Sariputra, the Bodhisattva, the Mahasattva Avalokitesvara, all those gathered, and all those of the world, the gods, humans, demigods, and the

*gandharvas were filled with admiration and
they all praised the Conqueror's words.*

. . .*gods* . . . .

In the exoteric sense *gods* refer to the
superior inhabitants of celestial realms; in the
esoteric sense *gods* can represent *siddhis* of higher
psychic powers and abilities and those of bodhi,
enlightenment.

. . .*humans* . . . .

This can refer to human beings on the Earth,
present at that time, or human beings in other realms
of the universe.

. . .*demigods* . . . .

These are lesser deities with minor godlike
qualities.

. . .*gandharvas* . . . .

These are celestial demigods, famed for their
musical skills. The name means "fragrance eater".
It is thought that they sustain themselves nutritiously
on fragrances.

. . .and they all praised the Conqueror's words.

"Well done", the Conqueror said three times. Everyone present agreed with the Buddha about the significance and vital import of the discoursed Heart Sutra just related by Avalokitesvara. It can be noted accordingly that truth applies in all realms, to all degrees of sensory ability, to all forms of conscious beingness, and to all intellectual and spiritual potential.

This completes the comments on The Epilogue.

CHAPTER 8

THOUGHTFUL REFLECTION

The Arising of Cintamayiprajna

With the completion of the study of the terms and their meanings used in the Heart Sutra, a broader and more penetrating review of their implications is now in order. While theories and conjectures can never provide proof of anything, thoughtful reflection and a deeper analysis can aid in the perfection of reason that can, at least, give a clearer indication of reality. Finding the truth and living in accord with truth is possible by exercising reason, once the right way of comprehending reality is found (right view), no more questions need be asked, and no more statements need be made regarding the matter. All the entanglements and delusions anyone experiences are due to ignorance, wrong knowledge, and lack of thoughtful reflection. But through the powers of reason these problems can be overcome.

The Heart Sutra is very short, very compact, and has broadly influenced Buddhist thought. It focuses primarily on the doctrine of sunyata, emptiness. The experience of emptiness is substantially different from knowledge that arises due to study, reasoning, or logical thinking. Yet these very steps are necessary as prerequisite for a direct understanding that will transcend the limitations of the discriminative intellect. Although the four lower aspects of prajna, sruti, cinta, bhavana, and niscaya have their arising from proper reason and analysis initially, adhiprajna results as the evolving fruition of wisdom. Adhiprajna is an integrated and holistic blossoming of wisdom, and leaves nothing uninspected. Yet this wisdom is beyond any function of intellect that uses descriptions, words, indications, or other symbolic tokens of expression such as analogies or similes. Thoughtful reflection is an extension of study and is necessary to further prepare the ground for insight that ultimately transcends reason and logic.

Sunyata, as found in Mahayana Buddhism, is the central and paramount doctrine around which all phenomena can be understood. Every effort, every means available at every available opportunity should be used to meticulously examine, understand and realize its implications. Everything that can be known as an objective phenomenon is subject to the application of the doctrine of emptiness. All objects and events are impermanent, have no inherent self, and are of the character of suffering. Whatever is commonly conceived as an individual object or person does not exist in the sense of its being a permanent, independent, or substantial individual.

Anatman means not-self. It is a specific Buddhist doctrine that defines a person as being empty of an eternal and changeless self-essence, sometimes referred to as a soul, often described as being an eternal soul, an aspect of selfness inhabiting the body. *Atman* (meaning self, soul), is a Vedic concept referring to an independent, unchanging and eternal identity. This identity as defined in this concept is the essential self-ness that is found at the very core of individuals and entities. It is thought to be the very essence of the particular form in which it finds a home. The implication behind this concept would be that these essential selves exist somewhere, in some warehouse of waiting selves, and become activated only when an appropriate body/form is available, and that after the demise of that body/form, it returns in its pristine, unchanging and unchanged form to home-central warehouse for whatever comes next.

Anatman, our Buddhist concept, finds its expression based on the teaching of interdependent origination; these creative steps in the process of all phenomenal conditions point to the fact that everything is impermanent, that everything is in a constant state of flux, and that everything draws on the interactions of other things in the becoming process. So if someone then identifies himself as being the five skandhas, or as being the body or the mind, this is simply called ego which is, even as a mistaken notion, also impermanent, changing and prone to suffering, a so-called personality made of component parts, structures that have no self either. No thing can be found that has a self-existing nature. Neither the mistaken human identity called ego nor any other quality or characteristic can be designated as a real self, a permanent and unchanging self-nature. This is exactly what Avalokitesvara comprehended when he *saw* that all five skandhas were empty of inherent existence.

The contemplative practitioner must penetrate into a thorough comprehension of anatman and understand that there is only a continuous process of arising and falling away in the phenomena considered mistakenly to be a separate ego, self, soul, or a permanently existing essentialness. There must be understanding that there is no self-existent individual or person who is behind the action of being, or at the center guiding this process, even though the common presumption is that this is generally the case. Because of the ongoing interdependent origination process functioning from a basic permeation of the seed of ignorance within the storehouse consciousness, the resulting mind-creations build and strengthen the memory until it takes on the role of the experiencing "I", and thereafter assumes its predominant role as a "self" experiencing all "others". This habitual assumption builds on and strengthens the individual idea of "self", and it might be fair to say that very few individual humans existing in the normal delusional state of awareness have some sort of feeling that "they" are not an eternal personality viewing "other" from behind their eyes and through their other sensory receptors. Very few will give any thought to the actuality of the matter or to the process that creates such an illusion.

The very concept of "eternal" requires there be an unchanging state of existence. It requires that whatever it is that is the complete whole-being exhibiting eternal qualities be so without change. The very idea of a separate and eternal soul-personality residing within a body, observing that body's thoughts, acts, etc., seems to be part and parcel of the taught assumptions of most religions. The dogma structure of religions also stresses in various ways the changing potentials for the individual person, stressing as part of the religious teachings the fact that change for the better is the way according to the teachings of their particular deity. The saving grace involved in this change process, after the "death" of the body, can then only be enjoyed if that eternal soul is able to exhibit those changes for the better of the personality involved in a state of being other than that which made the body possible. Such expectation-thinking is flawed, because an eternal soul, or anything whatsoever that is created, is incapable of being "eternal" since there is constant change taking place in all shape, form, and qualities. In our ignorance we usually do not consider such things, and if we do then the partial and errant expressions which language uses creates a jumble of mental formations that tend to finally end up in contradictory ideas. These ideas in their turn then create doubt and confusion which, when expressed, can quickly be put to rest under the comfort-blanket of "there are some things we can never understand and so must put our faith and trust in (place here your appropriate deity, cleric, guru, religious text, or whatever else gives solace).

So having now expressed what a "person" cannot be, let us explore what a "person" is. A "person" is a continuity of changing events, process itself, a complex flux of conditions that, when investigated, is all that a person really is. A collective set of conditions is not a self; it is not an isolated collectivity since all is related and interdependent, each with all, and all with each. A collective set of conditions is usually conceived of as a self, but there are only conditions, no real self-being or "eternal" entity of any sort. Albeit, this pseudo-entity, as a collectivity, does have the capability of altering the conditions of its collective conditionality, changing dysfunctional or unskillful characteristics into better ones, or vice versa. Since there is no definitive boundary anywhere in the totality of the flux of conditionality, there is nowhere that an isolated self can be found. All is process; all is functionality.

Without the recognition of this truth, one is left presupposing it is his ego personality that does good or ill, experiences suffering, gets enlightened or not, controls the doings of the body, oversees and does the doing; but it is not the ego personality, nor is it any kind of individual self that enters into the ultimate nirvana of the Heart Sutra discourse. In the Visuddhimagga, the great encyclopedic compendium of Theravada Buddhism, it is written:

There is suffering, but no sufferer is found;
Deeds are, but there is no doer;
Nirvana is, but no one who enters it;
The path exists, but there is no traveler of it.

The idea of an ego is another collective set of mental factors, and although there is some relative value in such conceptions, ideas are only ideas, always partial and in some degree faulty. The mind is faulty when it splits the phenomenal world into a perceiver and an object perceived. This is dichotomy, a presumption of a real duality between "me" as perceiver and the "other" as the perceived object. This initial dichotomy makes us think that everything and everybody are distinct and separate entities; thus the ego-notion "me" becomes a fixed conception which dominates the mind. Then attachment, desire, hate, greed, and more delusion arises, inevitably ending in some sort of suffering. This condition is healed and cut away by prajna-wisdom concerning the complete understanding of emptiness and selflessness.

Anatman and Sunyata are not so much philosophical or psychological principles or dogmas as they are instructional devices. All things, events, and objects (dharmas) are nothing more than collective appearances. As such they exist as objects perceived by sense organs and given mind-form, and resulting in patterned perceptual formats that can become more and more impressed, fixed, and ingrained. They are functional concepts of totality process, but as real and separate objects they are empty of any sort of permanent beingness; they exist as emptiness, and as being empty of inherent being they are non-existent.

The Heart Sutra does not make distinction between form and emptiness. Form is always a composite objectivity, and emptiness is a conceptual device. They both exist conditionally, form as a set of composites, and emptiness as a conditional thought structure related to that form. Verbal designations do not make something into a self. Language of any sort does not create a "self" when applied to a condition. Everything we experience in ignorance is thus mere definition, description, mental structure culminating in an act of naming, a composition of multitudes of interdependent factors. Buddhism uses the devices of anatman and sunyata to help the falsely discriminating mind cease its dysfunctions.

Everything is a ceaseless flux, a continuously changing event, but there is no definite thing that changes. Whatever is mistakenly conceived as an entity is only a set of conditions impinging on a sense faculty – which makes another set of conditions that we know as sense consciousness and sense data together with conditional elements. All of this is process interdependency, and there is no self at any location or point in time and space that is in any way separated from the entire process. What things are, as appearances, are abstractions made by mind, and the procedures of meditation can help reveal this. Things DO have a relative validity in terms of how they are referenced and comprehended and used, and there is a utility on the mundane level for the use of these concepts and verbal expressions, but what they describe are invalidities from the point of view of absolute truth. Real Truth (thusness) is emptiness.

All things are empty of a separate self-being (*svabhava*). Emptiness itself is also empty. There is no location where "empty" is found; there is no non-location where "empty" is found; there is no location where "not-empty" is found; there is no non-location where "not-empty" is found. Things are, and are not; change is, but no thing undergoes the change. The web of the conditional matrix is infinite and endless and all is its fuel, and there is no separation anywhere therein. Any separation that takes place, any object or event, so-called, is nothing

100

more than a conceptual "snapshot image" made by the errant mind that creates a semblance of selfhood out of a momentary small piece of the morphing process. What is called an object or a self, is only the aggregates doing what aggregates do, supporting the whole for their momentary existence, experiencing an instant in the flux, but mistakenly morphed into a separate mental item by the naming and defining mind. Use of words for descriptions of objects and conditions begins to lull us into a belief that there are real self-existent objects as these languages describe. We forget that words are arbitrary verbal absurdities used to describe perceptual absurdities, delusion based on primal ignorance.

Emptiness is a potent device used to counter the errant svabhava view. The differentiating way of conceptual awareness that sees things as having inherent selfness is the svabhava view, and it is so ingrained in consciousness that only skillful effort will undo the knot it has tied in our thinking. Understanding emptiness is the activation of prajna-wisdom, the prajna view that knows things as they really are, as selfless. In the Heart Sutra this is called practicing the Profound Perfection of Wisdom. The training is thoughtful reflection, a repetitive and successively deeper review of emptiness that can change the habitual memory-structure of the mind that comprehends according to the svabhava view. Thoughtful reflection is able to reverse memory patterns and can clear them away, allowing the pure prajna to function. The knot gets cut through. To awaken is to move beyond the deceptive dysfunction of the discriminating mind. Starting in lesser degrees the svabhava cognitions weaken and the prajna cognitions become more stable, and in time the svabhava perceptional process is completely overcome and replaced by pure prajna apperception. This is the mother of the buddhas.

Strong thought habits are established by repetition of certain kinds of thoughts. Habits of cognition can be overridden and replaced by ceasing the repetitive habit and replacing it with more skillful actions repetitively. The key is to understand that memory patterns can be changed; if they were self-existent they could not, as permanent self-entities, be changed. If we *see* the truth of emptiness, as did Avalokitesvara, we will awaken to ultimate nirvana, transcending all ills and suffering.

Sentient beings do not *have* buddha-nature; sentient beings *are* buddha-nature. This essential wisdom of purity gets covered over by traces of karma created by ignorant daily actions, interactions, all nurturing the svabhava viewpoint. As a result, beings are bound by the chains of this world in the rebirth circle (samsara), the wandering-on endlessly through the cycles of the effects of our thinking and deeds that arise conditionally according to our faulty discriminations. Fortunately, good advice comes to all by way of this Heart Sutra that gives knowledge to dispel obstructions to our buddhahood by dissolving patterns of erroneous cognition. Then the dust-covered mind can be cleansed and buddha-nature re-viewed.

Like Avalokitesvara, we can know the aggregates for what they are. They do not constitute a real "me"; neither do they or any object posses any inherent self-being. Form is emptiness and emptiness is form. No thing has any permanency; the only thing permanent is impermanence. Yet, neither impermanency nor change can be considered entities either because they are not of themselves, but function, process only. And these are only words, therefore empty, too. In this process of conceptual grasping and possessive clinging is the entanglement we encounter as turmoil and delusion. Only when we release the attachment to self, either personal self, or self in thing, will sublime insight and blissful awareness occur spontaneously.

It is possible to maintain precision awareness, a skillful and useful mind governed by right view and understanding, and by training in thoughtful reflection. If we can stabilize and maintain the prajna view we can remain free in the presence of truth-recognition beyond all distraction. Mental obscurations and conditional negative tendencies will lose their grip. To fulfill the training according to the Heart Sutra it is helpful to impress the text of the Sutra into memory. This is exactly why it is chanted over and over, century upon century, by the Buddhist congregation worldwide, as a contemplative and devotional practice. This is a radical pathway that can create the needed opening for an awakening from the deluded dream of ego and separateness. This delusional dream is the wheel of samsaric wandering. Whatsoever or whosoever desires to emerge from the bewilderments of the wheel, seeking the freedom of the bodhisattvas and the tathagatas, must study, reflect, meditate and act on the truth of emptiness and selflessness. It has been often said,

All things are impermanent;
All things are potentials for misery;
All phenomena are selfless;
Nirvava is peace.

Understanding this truth, coming to the recognition that the material and mental aggregates are all conditioned events, the misconception of a truly existent "me" gets abolished. The wheel of samsara and its consequential pain finds alleviation. Thoughtful reflection, training in correct view, seeing clearly and with reflection devoid of dust becomes an obvious necessity. Meditation gives final experiential certainty to this newfound Way. Upon this wisdom is found the nourishment for final and complete awakening. Upon this wisdom is found the engendering of the Perfections in their final brilliance.

CHAPTER 9

MEDITATION

The Arising of Bhavanamayiprajna

The Heart Sutra has given the methods for awakening through prajna-wisdom. These are the methods of the *"buddhas of the three times"*.

> We should study diligently to become knowledgeable in the definitive subject of the Sutra, emptiness.

> We should reflect upon the specifics of the knowledge yet more thoroughly and deeply.

> Meditation is practiced earnestly, supported by the knowledge thus acquired.

In Buddhism there are many ways described to reach bodhi and nirvana. In Mahayana scriptures these ways have been called the eighty-four thousand dharma doors, which means there are multitudes of ways to accomplish the task. Every way, specific and different, is an efficient method to be used by differing practitioners according to their varied capacities. Most fundamental in Buddhist meditational practices is the Noble Way taught by the Buddha based on the calming of the mind and realization of insights. This is called *samatha-vipasyana.*

Samatha means calming. *Vipasyana* means insight. These words have also been translated as tranquility and insight, stopping and seeing, calm and observation, and other similar renderings.

To calm the mind is to stop all scattering thought. To calm the mind is to inhibit the habitual working of discriminative functions of the mind. To calm the mind is to stop the processes practicing delusion and error. To calm the mind is to create new habits that purge the storehouse consciousness, bringing about less clouded perceptive functions, relief, and silence in samatha, a relaxed peacefulness with clarity of consciousness wherein rests a great potential for intelligence free from conceptual misconstructions and false views.

Vipasyana is insightful realization regarding purification of morality, concentration, and wisdom, all related to the Four Noble Truths with special emphasis on the Fourth Truth, the path leading to the cessation of suffering. With these are also the insights related to the three characteristics (*trilakshana*) of impermanence, suffering, and non-self. Insight into impermanence is the understanding of the conditions of change, of arising and of passing away. Insight into the characteristic of suffering is the realization of being oppressed by the facts of arising and passing away. Insight into non-self culminates in the abandoning of clinging to a self.

In addition to the above listed insights, there are also knowledgeable insights into other mind-creations such as aversion, attachment, detachment, extinction, desirelessness, emptiness, etc. When these insights are developed methodically, adverse conceptual views are vanquished and the mind is left without hindrances. Error is passed beyond. Nirvana is realized. Samatha-vipasyana is, according to Buddhist tradition, the core practice of all meditational procedures, and is cultivated through consideration and study of the Buddhist scriptures and treatises. Calm and Insight are equivalent with Concentration (samadhi) and Wisdom (prajna), which are the supporting structures for the practice of Meditation (bhavana). Concentration develops tranquility, a mind not agitated but serene and undistracted, with a quality of lucidity. Such calmness of mind is essential for deep development of insight. Samatha is one-pointed, vigilant attentiveness. Vipasyana is the correct view, the accurate and exact discrimination of phenomena as they really are. Samatha-vipasyana is the systematic *practice* that has a wide range of application, but always aims at the highest bodhi.

Samatha should not be practiced by itself, without vipasyana as its complementary balance, or vice versa. Each aspect supports the other. Some who meditate practice one method only and have been able to achieve "dry tranquility" or "dry insight", but both are supremely effective when used together. They are like twins, each reflecting the image of the other. The Buddha was not fully satisfied with the experience of samatha alone, but wanted full enlightenment. When he had carried to completion the calm one-pointedness of samatha he was then endowed with the capacity for vipasyana. These two together allowed prajna-wisdom to arise. When samatha was developed, the mind was developed; when vipasyana was developed all ignorance was abandoned. With ignorance thus dissolved the twelve-fold wheel of interdependent origination was disrupted and its functionality disintegrated.

The gateway allowing entry to the bodhi path is samatha-vipasyana, leading away from ignorance and toward wisdom. Samatha-vipasyana is not an easy undertaking, but a practitioner will be successful if persistent. Hindrances will be done away with; intelligence will grow into profound wisdom.

Keeping the precepts is a prerequisite for the practice of meditation. Avoiding the destructive influences arising from taking the lives of sentient beings, of taking away their necessary possession without permission, of using them for misdirected sexual purposes, for destroying their character by using falsehoods against them, and by destroying one's own mental clarity through the use of intoxicants, all these deter the achievement of awakened purity. Keeping the precepts is important in the breakup of the stream of primal ignorance, wrong thinking, and wrong behavior. Keeping the precepts is an important aid to concentration. The violation of the precepts prevents the overcoming of sorrow, grief, worry, anxiety, fears, and other related mind creations, and these in turn will always prevent a penetrating level of concentration from being achieved, thereby preventing any state of calm and insight being experienced.

The mind tends to become fixed on those aspects we call hindrances. There are five of them; lust, ill will, sloth and torpor, agitation and worry, and uncertainty. They are the supports for the distracting fascination of a wandering mind incessantly craving and seeking for gratification that by itself keeps the wheel of rebirth turning. When one who meditates has removed the obstructing five hindrances, his mind will be clear and lucid.

Another prerequisite is to take refuge in the Buddha, Dharma, and the Sangha. These are known as the three jewels of Buddhism, and taking refuge in them is a vow of trust that a teacher, a path, and a community is true and effective. Taking refuge is the primary reorientation of the ruling motivations of life, a shift in perspective away from base desires, and a move in the direction of bodhi.

When entering into any form of meditation, there are four physical postures that must be considered: sitting, standing, walking, and lying down. Because these are descriptions of general body postures during all living conditions, it is obvious that meditation can be done anywhere and at any time no matter what activity is being engaged in. Sitting meditation is the one used in most training situations, and is the more formal and exacting posture. For its use, the practitioner should, if possible, select a place as free as possible of disturbing distractions that might present difficulties for the meditation. When a place has been selected, sit down, cross the legs with one leg over the other leg, tucked in as tightly as is comfortable. Some find sitting on a few inch seat, feet being then lower, has helped. Should there be too much discomfort, as is usually the case in the beginning, such as pain in the knees, ankles, and hips, loosen up a bit. One does not want the meditation session to focus solely on the pain and agonies being experienced. There is nothing wrong with making the experience as comfortable as possible.

One hand is placed gently in the palm of the other hand, both resting comfortably in the lap of the practitioner. One should sit up straight, making the spine comfortable so as to support the head and neck and upper body without stress or pain. The general body condition should be such that when sitting there is comfort and relaxation achieved as the body remains braced and balanced so that the sitting session can be conducted with as little body motion as absolutely necessary for the duration of the session. Do not expect painless perfection the first time around. Mindfulness will ultimately achieve the right arrangement for every body attempting sitting meditation. One should not become lazy or careless. Dedication to each moment's needs must be maintained. Start with a few deep breaths, concentrate on the breaths, concentrate on normal breaths where the air is felt entering into and out of the nose. The basic preparations have now been made to begin the process of samatha-vipasyana.

The mantra found in the Heart Sutra is given as the expedient and skillful means for this process. By concentrating on the mantra and the repetition of it the attention is controlled. Miscellaneous or

113

disordered thoughts will cease to arise. Reciting the mantra with just an effort to continue the recitation can produce samatha. This calmness of mind is free from the influence of the hindrances, proclivities of an unruly mind locked into the habits of daydream, anxiety of sensual desires, or the moment to moment concerns and discriminations. This peaceful state of mind saves energy and displaces habitual patterns of karmic tendencies. The karmic seeds present in the alaya consciousness begin to be modified by more beneficial influences. The recitation of the mantra interrupts incessant mental chatter, and the habitual perspectives that perpetuate delusion are altered. When the fixated operations of the mechanical mind are shaken out of their structures by recitation of the mantra, the delusions they continuously propagate and support are cut through, and samatha begins to allow great stability. This is how the mantra is used for samatha.

The mantra need not be chanted continuously. Initially it should be used as many times as necessary to calm the mind. With practice fewer repetitions will be necessary to achieve samatha. When calmness of mind is being entered into, be aware of any stray thoughts that are arising, and if the mind is wandering, bring it back to the mantra. When no wandering thoughts enter into the meditative consciousness then the peaceful mental state of acute vigilant awareness IS samatha.

114

Should thoughts keep arising and the tendency to get lost in them also intrudes, just return to the recitation of the mantra for a few more recitations. Do this again and again. The mantra can be repeated whenever concentration wanes into distraction. When the mind is caught wandering, as mind tends to do, saying the mantra a few times reestablishes concentration and attentiveness.

Mantra recitation, when reflecting on its meaning, advances the practitioner in vipasyana so that insight into the emptiness of all phenomena is realized. Ceaseless recitation of the mantra is not necessary therefore, and focused concentration that will eliminate distracting thoughts can be achieved by mindfulness of the attributes making up the mantra. Its occasional use, as stated above, is to return the mind from a distracted state. It can also be used as an affirmation of trust in the Buddhadharma, staying with a correct view in the present moment. This mindful attentiveness must be developed with practice until thoughts are noticed at the very point of their arising. This is insightful meditative presence that heals the wandering mind of its habitual tendencies. This is how the mantra is used for vipasyana.

Samatha arises through a one-pointed focus on recitation of the mantra, and when ceasing the recitation samatha is maintained through a calm vigilance toward the potentially arising thought/mind. Samatha is basically stable and nonfabricated awareness; it is not distracted by arising memories or imaginings. Such creations are seen and understood with the onset of vipasyana arising atop the calm reflective mirror of samatha. The mantra becomes a support, a reminder; it is seed containing the full genetic structure of the Heart Sutra's message. Thus the mantra is "relied upon" and "bodhisattva mahasattvas should train in the Profound Perfection of Wisdom in just this way." Reflection on the meaning of the mantra restores the correct view. The steady strength is samatha as practice becomes skillful proficiency.

When conditioned thought arises it should be recognized as being a hindrance and obstruction to samatha, then released without discriminating mental activity. This is how insight works. Thoughts can be recognized as wholesome or unwholesome mental factors; they can be seen as the consequences of prior thoughts and actions that produce in their wake even more thoughts and actions of the same kind. Disengaging from the unwholesome aspects of thought fabrications is the "passing completely beyond all errors". The mantra, as can be seen, is a symbol that infers the insights contained in that which it represents. This makes the mantra equivalent to the knowledge gained through study, through thorough reflection, and through subsequent meditation, certainty, and the fullness of adhiprajna.

The mantra is an associative mnemonic tool to be used for deeply impressing one's understanding with a conclusive certainty. A thought, for instance, arising with the qualities of ill will, one of the five hindrances, is observed, recognized as the unwholesome factor it is but is not engaged with in mental dialogue. It is recognized as arising conditionally and so too will pass away conditionally. Seeing the thought in this way allows for its empty nature to be observed correctly, with no mental attachments constructed with regards to any notion of its having a permanent self of some sort, and in this state of clarity it is released, freeing the practitioner from any problematic karmic consequences it might otherwise create. While then applying some recitations of the mantra as a reminder of this correct view, *"they should correctly view the five skandhas also as empty of inherent existence."* The repetition of this meditative sequence over a long period of time produces a transformation of perspective from the svabhava view to the prajna view, the correct view.

Samatha-vipasyana is the arising of bhavanamayiprajna and is simultaneous with the cessation of superimposed mental elaborations. This mantra is a genuine protector of the mind, indicating

117

a contemplative presence with calm and insight, a profound device that can, when used rightly, aid in the remembrance that all is empty (*sarvam sunyam*). Prajna-wisdom becomes integral in the bypassing of mental hindrances and all they support. *"Because their minds are without hindrances, they are without fear."* The mantra is used like this for entering samatha, then samatha becomes a sturdy platform supporting insight. In the same way, the mantra is incorporated for maintaining stability in insight, the correct view. This is mnemonic training, practice.

The words of the Heart Sutra are negations of old and faulty ways of understanding, yet these negations are affirmations of the actual status of reality as it should be understood in the new way, the way a buddha sees reality. The Heart Sutra presents to us a marvelous and extraordinary method of deconstructing false views. The common status of the human mind is not quite as it should be, but by letting go of conceptual error the great net of delusion is rent and the truth is known: *"svaha"*, it is so! The mind can be free in bodhi, the state of not being deceived by something that does not really exist.

Everyone wants freedom and happiness, but everyone has not yet developed the skillfulness required, nor eliminated the unskillful qualities that hinder, so they remain in the prison of samsara, wandering-on through a subtle bewilderment, not knowing their real condition, and remaining prone to suffering. If somehow the unskillful qualities can be eradicated, beings can progress, but speedy development is rare. It is obvious that the Heart Sutra and its mantra indicate a developing progression from suffering to the cessation of suffering by passing completely beyond all errors, like cravings, attachments, and false views. When defilements and errors of the mind are recognized, mainly the predispositions behind a svabhava perspective, the wrong discrimination of things starts to fade away. Ignorance of emptiness gives stability to delusion but the reverse of this common situation is the prajna perspective, the absence of any notion of any self-being of any variety of phenomena. This is the correct view of the Heart Sutra, and it is the key leading to our escape from the yearning for that something that we seem unable to "put our finger on", yet which seems so important for us to discern.

The secret of the mantra is revealed to the contemplative by his prolonged and devoted use of it. Any who do not bother with reciting the Sutra and its mantra for the purpose of samatha, nor use the mantra for stable remembrance of correct view through insight, will not enter into deeper experience suggested by the Sutra. To all except the devoted practitioner the Heart Sutra remains an obscure and abstract text. In order to grasp its profound meaning and the pragmatic use of its mantra, one must become exceptionally and thoroughly familiar with it, pursuing the meditational process it indicates by repeatedly dwelling on the implications of emptiness and completing the path that the Sutra and mantra embody. The Heart Sutra must remain somewhat of a mystery to all except the practitioner who learns to see into his own prajna where truth is finally revealed.

The samadhi *"perception of the profound"* is pure vision, unclouded understanding, true gnosis, errorless, and total absence of all delusion. The mantra is paradoxical in that it indicates a path progressively traveled, but there is nothing to be attained along the way. The real path is a progressive LOSS of delusion. There is no "movement" either, a going from some place to someplace else, as movement is usually thought of. This kind of movement must be negated also. The real movement is a "going" into progressive realization of where one actually is already, finally realized when delusion has been eliminated, bit by bit, from the mental equation. The movement, *"gate"*, is the deconstruction of those propensities within the discriminating mind that are the basis for superimposing overlays and confusions onto objects of perception. *"Nothing to attain"* is the realization that what is sought, namely cessation of suffering et al, is present already, but this fact is revealed only gradually as one passes progressively *"beyond all error"*, when suddenly one arrives knowingly at the point where one has always been but could not distinguish because of the dust obscuring clear reflection of reality.

"Gate", move to eliminate constricted attention. The abstract idea found in this term is that attention to the mantra is a singular willful movement of attention (*gamana*) away from all that distracts; moving attentively, prajna is arising; *"gate"*, keep moving this way, away from fixations and inattentiveness; *"paragate"*, moving beyond all hindrances, prajna is clearing the understanding; *"parasamgate"*, moving even beyond all ideas of movement or one's self-being who moves, beyond all error, all aspects of prajna together in certainty of clear understanding.

To enlarge the discussion, *"gate"*, is the moving toward final cessation of ills and suffering, toward a prajna view, transcending all conventional categories of mundane knowledge, all categories of supramundane knowledge, and beyond into unsurpassed knowledge, the knowledge of those who have "to thusness gone" (tathagata). Such is the power of *"the great mantra, the unsurpassed mantra"*. The prajna perspective is the clear and unpolluted perspective, without the limitations of lesser conventional knowledge capable of describing only partialities. Prajna perception is not fixated on any partiality, but is open and free, with the wisdom of emptiness. This is bodhi, and the culminating point for the fullness of prajna (adhiprajna) view, the awakening *out* of the movement binding one to ignorance and all hindrances, awakening *into* the movement of unbinding, nirvana.

"Svaha!" It is true; it is so! This is the final affirmation, the truth of total perfect understanding, the commitment to reality, the bodhi-vision of a buddha, a totally integrated shift in perspective, the knowing of the dynamism of the totality of the phenomenal continuum.

Thinking about the unified totality of the matrix of thusness as a contemplation subject, done repeatedly over a regular period of time, crystallizes the understanding, making deeper and more fully established impressions. Meditation, with the use of this mantra so intimately associated with the path to bodhi, emptiness, and the movement to thusness, is a means of internalizing truth/reality through a remembrance device. In an advanced state of practice using the mantra, a question should be asked, "Who is reciting the mantra?" This question turns attention around on itself, the ultimate introspective introversion, attentiveness toward who it is that is being attentive; prajna seeing into itself.

This is buddha-mind realizing itself as selflessness, the final movement beyond. It is like peeling an onion, one layer after another removed until the center is revealed. And there is no thing there.

It is thus, *"tadyatha"*.

This mantra proceeds from the state of existence called error to the state of existence called bodhi by showing a progression, not through stages of attainment or accomplishment, but through stages of "letting go" of false views. This is an activity of the present moment, a movement in the eternal now. *"Gate"*, let go, going; *gate*, let go more, keep going; *"paragate"*, let it all go, keep going beyond; *"parasamgate"*, let go even of the concept of letting go, of someone who lets go, of something to let go of; everything is interdependent, together, empty of self-being. Just be *bodhi*; it is so, *svaha!* This is the movement of prajna called bhavana. The movement is then later completed with certainty and with fullness.

CHAPTER 10

CERTAINTY

The Arising of Niscayamayiprajna

Study and thoughtful reflection are generally sufficient for gaining inferential certainty in understanding emptiness, but meditation is a further necessity for completion of the transition from inference to direct and immediate knowing. With practice a deepening meditation gives more than just an intellectual certainty. Direct perception, although supported by analytical studies, transcends those supports and completes them when meditation becomes more and more constant and stable. Perfect certainty regarding the truth of emptiness comes about by repetitious review of prior studies and then through meditation the knowledge is applied to the operations of the mind, ascertaining the correct view about how things really exist by ascertaining how they do not exist, and then making the proper adjustments in the thinking process.

Things may appear differently to a more cultured perceptive capacity through meditational insight, and will be known with ultimate certainty when direct experience and clear discrimination give the proof. That which cannot be directly experienced for the time such as nirvana, rebirth, or enlightenment, must be subjected to reasoning and subsequent valid inference. Neither can emptiness be directly experienced at first without a good supporting structure of reason and analysis. But when thoroughly cultivated in meditation, the correct view that all things are empty can erupt into a direct and profound non-inferential, and non-connectional, understanding, a *"perception of the profound"*.

One of the best ways to cultivate a more extensive and complete understanding of emptiness is through an examination of the idea of the two truths, relative truth (*samvritisatya*) and ultimate truth (*paramarthasatya*). The mundane relative truth is the way things appear to be, taken by the common run of human awareness to be real and appearing in manifested form through causality. The transcendent ultimate truth is that everything is empty of self-being. This truth cannot be perfectly expressed through the terms and concepts of language, but can be experienced directly. Although not specifically mentioned in the text of the Heart

Sutra, the two truths are nevertheless represented by "form" (the relative truth) and by "emptiness" (the ultimate truth).

The difference between the various Mahayana Buddhist schools is usually merely a difference in the way the two truths are explained, and the way emptiness can be understood and experienced. In meditation the practice is with the movement of thought merged with the application of the wisdom of emptiness; each thought is empty and is part of a process of interdependent origination, as are all phenomenal objects and events. Form as relativity and emptiness as ultimacy may seem to be two different things, a dichotomy. But meditation on, or analysis of, either one exclusive of the other inevitably leads to an imbalanced focus and viewpoint. Any perceptible object is always relatively existent; there is something there which exists – but the object is also empty; it represents emptiness. The two truths are both valid simultaneously.

"Form is emptiness and emptiness is form."

It is not possible to abandon the reality of the appearance of form, nor is it possible to deny its inherently empty nature. Neither of these two aspectual truths can be excluded from their one source. Each has the other as its basis of existence. All relativity is like illusion since there is no singular separate entity anywhere, and no thing can be investigated or even defined without relating it to other appearances; hence the definition of relativity as something which exists is only contingent with the existence of something else. Appearance as such must be real or there would be nothing to designate as objectively empty. Emptiness as concept depends upon form, and has no separate existence apart from form, therefore emptiness cannot be an entity either; it is also selfless in the same way as form is selfless. Form and emptiness are not separate and distinct, not a distinctly separate dichotomy. The way a bodhisattva mahasattva or a buddha sees reality is by way of the two truths, both fused into an holistic view, a profound and perfect truth. When meditation advances, the svabhava apprehension has to be passed beyond because the two truths are no longer mistakenly presumed to be two different things.

> *"O Sariputra, form is none other than emptiness and emptiness is none other than form. Form is emptiness and emptiness is form."*

When the Heart Sutra defines the two truths in this way it is to be taken as the correct way to view things. One of the clearest formulas elucidating this view was the doctrine of the threefold truth used in the T'ien Tai, the Hua Yen, and the Yogacara schools of Buddhism. This doctrine says:

(1) The absolute truth is that all phenomena are empty of their own specific selfhood since they all arise dependent on condition.

(2) The relative truth is that having a temporary appearance, all phenomena are interdependent and relative and are thus conventionally valid.

(3) The two truths are both aspects of reality, and in correct meditation both truths must be recognized together simultaneously, fusing them into one all-comprehensive, holistic, non-conceptual apperception.

This simultaneity of prajna-vision is the esoteric meaning of *parasamgate* in the Heart Sutra's mantra that takes one, through study and reflection beyond into meditation, until certainty, the apperception that the relative and the ultimate are not separate, and until *"Form is emptiness and emptiness is form"*, is known directly.

Meditating upon one of the two truths, and then upon the other alternately, is a format for analytical knowledge. When a practitioner actually realizes the integral truth of form and of emptiness without switching from one to the other, one moves beyond the negations of emptiness and the affirmations of form, beyond the dualism of relative and of ultimate, *parasamgate*. The practitioner realizes that everything perceived through the senses and comprehended with the mind is like a dream; this is an awakening to reality as it really is. Many times in Prajnaparamita Sutras it is said,

> *"As a star, a visual aberration, a lamp, an illusion, dew, a bubble, a dream, lightning, and a cloud – view all composites as such."*
> (The Diamond Sutra)

Looking at the world from the standpoint of svabhava perception is partial and errant perception mixed with superimposed conceptual classifications with reference to ego-notions and selfhood. That is why it is like a dream, a dream of the uncultivated mind; it is also like a dream because there is no thing substantial in it. Awakening to the standpoint of prajna-wisdom where there is certainty of understanding in spontaneous presence we can remain in the absence of false discrimination and constructed identification with the skandhas. What is usually taken as normal perception and cognition is, in fact, a state of false understanding in which nearly everyone abides constantly when they fail to inspect their mental mechanisms and recognize the truth of things as they really are. Enlightening texts such as the Heart Sutra always suggest inspection and analysis of our inner and outer worlds, and awakening to the real nondual situation. Even the "inner" and the "outer" are mere conceptual designations and are not two in reality because dharma cannot be one-sided. If one side is denied then the other side is automatically affirmed and if the opposite choice is taken then the opposite is the result. This is the way the mind habitually splits one reality (*dharmata*) into a relative pseudo-dualism.

There is a possible misunderstanding of an apparently basic contradiction in the formula for interdependent origination that is pointed out in the Heart Sutra. Form happens to be a product of the origination process which is an affirmation of being.

But emptiness negates only form's self-being. The Sutra does not negate the being of form according to the process of conditional arising, but only negates its self-beingness. So being is non-being, and non-being is being. Even "affirmation" and "negation" are a duality that dissolves when prajna-wisdom cancels out the dichotomizing mind. Understanding only the phenomenal side, which interdependent origination in its twelve phases presents, is a partial and dualistic discrimination. Non-dual apperception, however, transcends the partial view, and completes it. This was the task of the Heart Sutra being spoken on Vulture Mountain so long ago. The view of prajna-wisdom is a re-unification of a split that should never have been, a re-integrated view of the way reality really is and always has been, a healing of the disunity of dualistic perception.

"Appearance" is a term denoting objective form, that which something "seems to be" in the absence of prajna apperception of what something really is. This apperception must accord with the realization of the truth of sunyata as authoritatively taught in the Heart Sutra to the point where even terms and concepts with their structural limitations and imperfect capabilities are put into proper perspective. "Emptiness" is a term describing the true condition of form, defining it as not what it may seem to be but pointing out its conditional absence of selfhood. Appearance and emptiness each engender the other. There is no separating them. They go together as part of the true perceptual experience.

If we inspect our true condition we may eventually awaken to the fact that we have long been under the influence of a habitual presupposition that everything emerges into existence as a result of strict causation, perhaps from a creator entity of some sort, and that an individual is a totally autonomous being. These presumptions are hidden away and unquestioningly accepted in the minds of nearly every human. Only those who undertake contemplative introspection will uncover these notions and become aware of the depth to which they distort perception and knowledge. When much is learned about conditioned mental factors, their operations, and how they interrelate in the cognition process, then it will, with certainty, be known that serial cause and effect as usually perceived, is only appearance, a seeming reality to those who have not yet correctly understood the conditional arising and therefore inherently temporary state of form-ness, emptiness. Causes and effects are not self-existent entities.

Abiding in the Noble Middle Way is a balance between these two truths, just in the middle, with no distinction between them as being separate realities. A perfect fusion is equanimity, a prajna perspective of fullness, of totality. All dichotomies should be resolved through rigorous contemplative practice in order that that which was previously partially understood will be truly seen and fully comprehended. This is a radical transformation.

Understanding is polluted when the dichotomizing mind has adopted habitual patterns to the level of reactive mechanical conditioning. This patterning of the mind is the unnoticed format and filter through which all perceptions and concept-creations are formulated. Untainted discernments become tainted through the mind's additions or subtractions resulting from these erroneous consciousness habit-seeds. Dichotomous perception occurs when the dysfunctional non-lucid mind divides objects and events into supposed separate singularities conceptually removed from their actual integral relationships in the functional unity of the realm of reality *(dharmadhatu)*. Since there is no such thing as a separately originating, separately existing, or self-produced phenomena, the dichotomizing intellect is obviously errant in its dualistic suppositions. Deluded ideas of self-existence are based on mechanical suppositional mental formulas that add to and leave out basic verities. The vision that fuses the two truths is prajna-vision, and certainty (niscaya).

Dualistic and partial perception is chronic delusion, the non-understanding of the two conjoined truths. By not understanding the mental process of attachment and identification, and the consequent mistaken notion of separateness, the notions of the "me" and "other" become fixed perspectives, and this kind of habitual mental fixation gets so deeply ingrained that thinking and activity fall below the level of conscious awareness and into subconscious automatism. The individual then becomes regularly absorbed in the compulsive and reactive processes of mental, emotional, and physical arenas of experience. Being absorbed means being engrossed, captivated and locked perpetually into inattentive modes of passivity and distraction. The interdependent chain of events generated by this delusive absorption leads always to conflict, misery, turmoil, and suffering. And it does so as a result of the associated train of thought that continues mechanically in the non-lucid mind of the one experiencing.

All discernible events are temporary when judged with an isolated relativistic view. Objects and events are extant only as a perceivable movement within the flux of conditioned factors, none of which have any substantial fixed existence when judged with prajna-wisdom. Disruption of absorption within aberrational thought processes is critical for the seriously devoted practitioner. It is begun by the process of samatha, creating gaps in the flow of inattentiveness that allows undisciplined thoughts to fight for dominance and attention. Short moments of attentiveness disrupt habitual inattentiveness. Creating habitual attentiveness eventually eliminates inattentiveness and becomes the perceptive "way". Inattentiveness in the mental process results from the dualistic concept of the "ego" notion of a permanent and eternal self, and the "self-being" notion of all "other". With the stabilization of attention and with certainty of understanding, samatha-vipasyana accomplishes lucidity and the elimination of delusion and distraction.

Here is the all-comprehensive truth: *"Form is emptiness and emptiness is form"*. The sense windows of our consciousness give the appearance of substantial being to that which is contacted though those apertures. But the result of this creative process is not that which was the contacted object of these sensory aggregates as one mistakenly assumes the "other" to be, but is only the mental creation resulting from the aggregate creative components reflecting in mind. True reality is that which is NOT what one creates. Freedom results from living non-discriminatively. Samsara becomes nirvana, and nirvana becomes samsara.

CHAPTER 11

FULLNESS

The Arising of Adhiprajna

Adhiprajna is the height of prajna and its fullness: The classic Buddhist description of prajna-insight is metaphorical, like a clear mirror with the ability to reflect and reveal all things just as they are. The clearness of the mirror corresponds to clarity of perception with no obscuration due to mental qualities. When prajna functions in its fullness, perception also reaches its perfection, seeing things as lacking identity, lacking permanent and inherent characteristics, and originating only in interdependence with multitudes of conditions. The thusness of existence cannot be fully realized through logic or reasoning alone, but can be understood through rigorous and persistent practice, along with previous analytical reflection. Meditation practice allows a radical purification of perspective, dissolving the dichotomous views of svabhava.

Thusness is a designation for "what is, as it really is". Things are only what they are, not what they may seem to be in conjunction with the conceptual imputations overlaying them as part of their being cognized. Thusness refers to reality (dharmata) as it actually exists; form is emptiness and emptiness is form. The real primordial nature of mind, when it is clear like the mirror and unobstructed by delusion and distraction, is also called thusness or "thusness of mind". Buddha-nature (tathagatagarbha) also equates with thusness of mind, as does the realm of reality (dharmadhatu). Dharmadhatu is the realm of phenomena as well as the realm of principle underlying phenomena. There is no incompatibility between one thing and another because all things are emptiness and have an identical reality. The highest insight is the simple and unadorned cognition of things in their natural thusness, being naturally "just thus". Thusness is inconceivable in the absence of the operative fullness of prajna-wisdom, adhiprajna. The vision of thusness cannot happen just through theory or speculation but can be a fully realized and constantly lived reality. The central intention of the Heart Sutra is to qualify the aspirant in this Profound Perfection of Wisdom.

Thusness is also equivalent with the Four Noble Truths as describing the way things really are. Thusness is also a term embracing essential consciousness, the beginninglessness and endlessness of all objects and events, and the selfless empty nature of all phenomena. Nothing has any self-identity apart from the oneness of thusness; everything is an aspect of thusness. What we add to something as part of our cognitive ramblings do not in reality give a thing any permanent selfness. There is only thusness whether it is realized or not. Even descriptions of thusness are only thusness, which means they are only as they are, descriptions only. If we understand, there is thusness and understanding of thusness; if we do not understand, there is still thusness and the presence of non-understanding – which is also thusness. The knowledge of thusness is adhiprajna and that culminates in bodhi. Those who realize thusness are called Tathagatas. The direct realization of the interdependent origination of all and everything is the mind of thusness.

The mind of thusness also sees interdependent origination as a description; all is just description until description is also realized as true thusness. The true thusness of mind conjoins with the universe of true thusness; the relative and the ultimate are seen as a unity. All is thus, as-it-is. There is no interference between form and emptiness and there is no barrier between the two truths. Waves in the ocean cannot be isolated from the ocean; the ocean is differentiated into waves only descriptively, conceptually. Waves are the same as the ocean, but they do have difference, but the difference and the sameness must be fused together in the mind of thusness. There is no real duality anywhere.

The real nature of phenomena is nonduality and emptiness; the dharmadhatu is thusness. No single object or event has its own self-essence, so not two things can be ultimately different since they are both merged in thusness. The flux, the process, and all functions within the totality of existence are the matrix of thusness. There is nothing outside the matrix; it is all inclusive. There is no thing that can be accurately or completely described and defined by limited language because characteristics are infinite. Therefore, the dharmadhatu is inconceivable, beyond conceptual elaboration, beyond the discriminations of the mind. But thusness is not beyond the mind of thusness because they are the same. Thusness can realize itself because that is its inherent potential, buddha-nature. One in whom this process has come to its fullness is called "one who to thusness has gone".

All manifested appearances of objects and events are always simultaneously the same in their real identity of thusness, no matter what the apparent temporal differences and characteristics may seem to be. The thusness of anything is the same as the thusness of anything else. The interdependence of all phenomena is as it is because, ultimately, any one thing depends for its existence on all else, and all depends on each one, whether remotely or immediately. Without thusness there is no existence whatsoever.

The mind of thusness sees all as already perfected. Objective interdependent structures are thusness manifestations; all arises exactly as it does, exactly as it should, according to conditional patterns. Dharmadhatu is functional perfection; whatever happens is a result of potentiality previously objectified in prior patterns. Egoistic efforts are always directed toward an alteration of something conceptually deemed imperfect or unacceptable. This is the mundane way of understanding, but in the supramundane perspective all polluted mundane knowledge is transcended, and what is conditional and empty is seen as it is, and motivations to alter conditions are abandoned in favor of a return to lucid awareness. When all aspects of the existential matrix of being is known as operating in perfection, then the contemplative can begin to become more stable in that knowing presence, liberated from the bonds of aberrant imaginations and superimposing projections. This is the unsurpassed knowing presence, spontaneous and beyond conceptual entanglements, beyond "*all ills and suffering*" based on the cravings of ego-based motivations. This spontaneous presence is the absence of delusion, the absence of hindrances, the realm of tathagata, the unsurpassed holistic knowledge based on emptiness, the mind of thusness.

The particular import of the Heart Sutra is that the universe of phenomenal manifestation should be understood from the position of bodhi, enlightenment. We live in the samsaric existence, but unknown to most it is identical to the inconceivable dharmadhatu. Samsara and nirvana cannot be separated; samsara is nirvana and nirvana is samsara. The only difference between the two is that in samsara ignorant beings are attached to ego-motivated activities through self-identification, whereas bodhisattva mahasattvas and buddhas are not. The two realms, samsara and nirvana, lokadhatu and dharmadhatu, the relative and the

144

absolute, phenomena and noumenon, are seen as merged, fused, conjoined, and nondual by the Buddha. What is real also includes the facts of suffering and delusion as well as the fact of enlightenment; all are functional aspects of thusness.

To presume that enlightenment is the complete and total knowledge of all details of everything will produce a motivation to attain all possible knowledge. Of this the human mind is incapable. The mind gathers in partial details and characteristics of things through sense contact, and then compares qualities and discriminations. The human mind is limited, while details of knowledge are limitless because of the limitless change and infinite motion taking place within conditional perpetual flux. Reality cannot be known through any intellectual construct; reality is known only through identity with it. This means it is crucial to disassociate with conceptual error. Bodhi is necessarily beyond conventional knowledge, yet inclusive of it and incorporating it into an all-inclusive holistic recognition of thusness-reality. The relative cannot be excluded in a correct, holistic view of ultimate reality beyond all concepts. To try to conceptualize what is too vast to be conceivable by the discriminating mind is to quit the race one step short of the finish line.

Freedom from the apparent bondage of conditional restraints of the samsaric wandering-on comes about through a comprehensive understanding in cognition with a fullness of experiential direct realization. Understanding the totality of the matrix of existence, life and events in inconceivable flux, is the mind of thusness. All the boundless fluctuations of perceptual conditionality are spontaneous modifications and adjustments of thusness in its manifestations of potentiality. There can be no thing related to thusness as an "other" and there can be no true comprehension of thusness as a separated "many", or a oneness without its many "others". There is nothing but this thusness and naught else than it. The totality of manifestations, as phenomena, along with that which perceives the manifestations, arises and disappears, assembles and disintegrates, as a spontaneous morphing of infinite conditional relationships. Neither can the flux, nor thusness, nor the mind of thusness be considered as an independent, self-existing thing, or being unto itself.

The whole cosmos is implicit in every one of its parts, just as waves are identifiable as ocean. The universe is a dynamic and holistic movement, and when a contemplative has subdued the dichotomous tendencies in his discriminative mind he gets a feeling of cosmic oneness of all things and beings. This feeling arises when there is an absence of the ego-notion, and it is this feeling that is the basis for the compassionate idealism exercised by buddhas and bodhisattvas. The matrix of events is constantly changing and in a process of generation, growth, and decline in each of its parts. A bodhisattva or a buddha with unsurpassed knowledge of the nature of the matrix of thusness can replace belligerence with kindness and compassion, change the unwholesome into wholesomeness, or create environments that help beings transcend their problems. The dharmata (reality) thus becomes malleable for those who study, reflect, and practice, who realize emptiness and the mind of thusness, bodhi. Each mind can and does have the power to change the field of the matrix for good or for ill. Deluded beings can transform conditions for ill and for degeneration, while bodhisattvas vow to deliver beings from ill. Thus our world is the kind of world that it is, a *saha* world, a world of endurance. Conditions endure according to the minds that create them.

The dimensions in which we flay about are apparitional projections and distorted reflections of a basic reality so inconceivable that we can only imagine what the truth of it may really be like. The reality we think we see is a partial perception, a mediocre facsimile of a grandiose thusness. Appearances and phenomena are not false; they are real, but they are usually perceived in a false manner. Perceivable dimensions of existence, if observed as a holographic system, will appear more clearly as what they really are. Coincidences, accidents, and synchronicity are then subjects susceptible to logical exploration as events coinciding dependent on the continuum of the conditions in the matrix of thusness. Things can be individual parts of a continuum of undivided wholeness, being the wholeness itself yet retaining individual uniqueness. Nothing is ever separately unique because the concept of uniqueness depends on comparison with "others". The ongoing misconceptions of things as separately "self" and "other" are the fault of the discriminating mind. In actualizing the correct view by way of the fused two truths, every supposedly single thing is then known as a subtotality complex, a speck of color in a mosaic of infinity. Within relativity is a static essence of thusness, of absolute holism, and a dynamism of interwoven functions and processes that are the matrix, a fused oneness-and-multiplicity, homogeneity-and-heterogeneity in perfect fullness.

Consciousness in the individual is just ordinary wakeful awareness interacting with the supposed differentiations of the manifested world. In its unobstructed and unconfined state consciousness has a natural lucidity. This clarity is the original face, the primordial, conditionless condition of free and pure consciousness, the mind of thusness. The individual contemplative, once having recognized his natural holistic presence, is then concerned with integrated wholes, or the total system of manifestation within the phenomenal matrix, rather than with deluded absorption in and attachment to the supposedly separate parts of it. All phenomena are then recognized as they really are, as interrelated components of the unified field of ever-changing conditionality. In undifferentiating, nondual holistic lucidity (bodhi) all the implications of the afflictions of conceptual dualism have ceased to be and the phenomenal matrix is clearly observed and understood.

CHAPTER 12

BODHI SVAHA!

There are many ways of expressing an idea. Dialectic is one format which has proven very efficient and it is sometimes presented as a discussion using logic and reasoning in a dialogue, or through question and answer, as a systematic investigative procedure. Our Heart Sutra has used this sort of question and answer to good effect as a method of disciplining the power of reason for philosophic and spiritual realization. Certainty is the requirement; theory and conjecture can never prove anything and can only provide possibilities. But dialectic can deliver us to a more perfect reason and clarity of thinking by analysis through which, at the very least, reality can be indicated. Prajna-wisdom is the superb virtue of the paramitas and can be induced through the use of dialectic as a means to determine the validity or invalidity of any question, any statement, or any answer. "Dia" means "through" or "across", dividing something into two parts, or investigating something from two different standpoints in order to expose wrong and incomplete conclusions and see the deceptions of an errant mind that lets one sink into illusion, hypnosis, bias, and even insanity. The dialectic method can cut through delusion by investigation into language, which provides descriptions through the use of opposite terms or by association with similarities. So each concept provided by language becomes mind-structured and dualistic. The method of the Heart Sutra transcends even the best logic because logic becomes contradictory since it is limited to the mental categories of dualistic language. Because any statement always uses a term or terms that are supported by their opposite term, any affirmation of what something is can be understood only in a relative and dependent context with its implied opposite term – or what something is not, apoha. In this way, any statement has to be understood by what it is not. Thus, one must finally admit ignorance of understanding what something really is since it can only be defined by what it is not. Reality is beyond any format of expression by language or conceptual elaboration because reality does not have an opposite and cannot be defined by what it excludes. Reality is perfectly all-inclusive.

Another way to express an idea so that a realization can "go beyond" the limitations of logic is through the use of paradoxical language. Any kind of a statement or proposition, insofar as it may be presented as an attempt to define reality, will be found to contradict itself. For example, this statement: "Reality is absolute, infinite, unbounded." Absoluteness, however, excludes whatever is limited, partial, incomplete, or separate. So then, absoluteness must exclude limited objective relativity, and exclusion is the obvious standard for limitation, or what something is not. Exclusion is a delineation of an excluding boundary between two things – what is supposedly there and what is not there. Thus, absoluteness sets conceptual boundaries. Calling the absolute "unbounded" becomes a contradiction because the absolute has to be thought of as unlimited – which excludes all limitation. As relative phenomena each have boundaries and limitations, they cannot be termed absolute and must be excluded from the definition. But in actuality, there is nothing excludable from the absolute; it is absolutely absolute. In the same way, infinity must actually include all finite phenomena, which appears paradoxical.

Once we find the right way, the skillful means, of seeing reality, no more questions and statements and answers need be made. The usual forms of concept-making are the very limitations which create the obstructions in the first place. So here in our Heart Sutra we find paradoxical statements that go against the grain of conventional language and thought. Why should we try to attain prajna-wisdom or bodhi when the Sutra tells us there is *"no attainment"*? The paradoxical language of the Sutra is intended to unite the opposites of conditioned relative reality and the ultimate truth, thusness, or the absolute truth. There seems to be a tension between the two truths, relative and absolute. This is because conventional language and conventional thought separates everything through a mind that grasps each thing in terms of its distinct characteristics. The Sutra tells us there is no difference between form and emptiness which is the same as saying there is no difference between the relative and the absolute. The absolute is unconditioned, yet it has to also include the totality of conditioned states. So when the truth is realized it is because mind can only conceptually grasp relative and conditioned form, but because form is not separate from the absolute truth, thusness, then the ultimate truth is indicated through conventional form, which is also thusness.

Prajna is an in-seeing or a direct and immediate knowing, an *experience* of emptiness. This is completely different and beyond any sort of conceptual fabrication, perception, or knowledge which is "attained" through reasoning, philosophical thinking, or logic. The Heart Sutra teaches about a trans-conceptual *experience* that is beyond anything that could be revealed or indicated through words, symbols, or ideas. It is this prajna-wisdom that dissipates all mental delusion, the mother who gives birth to all bodhisattvas and all buddhas.

There is a mystical profundity in this Perfection of Wisdom that shows us the fact that all phenomena are empty of their own substantial self-existence. The revelation is that all sentient beings are *already* beyond the limitations of self-existence and all the stress of entanglement within the world process. There really is nothing to attain. Striving and seeking are ego-based and will only keep the wheel turning. Identifying oneself with the skandhas is the primal mistake, the ignorance of emptiness. Only by *seeing* into the truth of it all, as did Avalokitesvara, will it be possible to jump off the wheel.

Everyone has gradually accumulated habitual notions of ego and separation. The dichotomizing way of the common intellect has become the standard, and this becomes the base for disharmony and the continuity of lack of true discernment. So to become aware of how and why misconceptions originate is the way to be free from deluded thought. When someone is able to get the vision, or *see* that which is beyond all thought, then he moves through prajna-wisdom to bodhi. Ordinary beings have so far not proceeded along the right path, so they are tangled in a continuous stream of conceptual delusion, never free from dichotomous thoughts. If someone reaches to insight into that which transcends the thought stream, then he knows how and why deluded thoughts arise, and he also knows he is that which is beyond thoughts. He comes to know he has been existing as a mistaken identity, fulfills the skillful means used to put an end to the deluded thought stream, and manifests prajna-wisdom and bodhi.

All phenomena have the same essential nature, that is, each phenomenon is empty of its own self-existence. All phenomena are nondual, meaning that apparent diversity is only an illusory appearance. In whatever way any thing may seem to appear, its real essential nature cannot differ from every other thing (dharma), and this sameness is not concept but the true fact of nonduality. All phenomena are beyond any sort of thought fabrication because the limited human mind is not capable of conceiving correctly all the details and characteristics of everything in existence, of all the infinite causal and relative correlations and endless potentialities and possibilities inherent in the totality of conditional relations. What is ultimately real is beyond thought constructs since it is both immanent and transcendent, within and beyond each particular objective form. Elaboration by means of concepts and ideas cannot ever truthfully or completely represent the infinity of form or emptiness. The one word that indicates this inconceivability is "thusness".

We do not have to create or change anything; all that is necessary is to just recognize our real essential nature of thusness, of what-really-is, and *see* all as-it-really-is. What is beyond and behind our nearly incessant thoughts is the unaltered state of awareness, the amalavijnana, or the mind of thusness. Alterations and corrections in the thought processes are functions of the dichotomizing mind absorbed in the delusion of dualisms. Whether pertaining to conscious awareness or to phenomena, thusness means things as-they-really-are. When we examine the primal, unaltered state of awareness, we are re-identified as what-we-really-are, the mind of thusness. This is the state of being Avalokitesvara was in when he *saw* that the five skandhas were empty.

When the true state of phenomena or mental factors are closely examined, it is found that without exception all are empty. Everything is stamped and sealed with the truth of thusness and no thing can be excluded from thusness. True thusness permeates all places without boundaries; reality is thusness-essence, always retaining its own nature without change. Its nature is the self-essencelessness of all things. The mark of true thusness is markless, signless, non-conceptual, and unconnected to any limit of boundary or realm, yet the nature of thusness always adapts and establishes sentient beings. Thusness is omnipresent, eternally pure, and pervades all times, but cannot be explained in words. Thusness is not something that can be cultivated or attained.

When everything is realized and experienced as pure thusness already, there is no need to cling or act upon ego-based motivations. All is in harmony already; everything is as it should be because of the causal chain. Mental contractions, called thoughts, are just fabrications so there is no need to get absorbed in the delusion of them; just stay in the unfabricated state. This is a spontaneous continuity of presence and can be known in one's primal being. Freedom from the influence of mental constructs is the freeing of constricted attention, the de-programming of constriction habits. This is the entry into the heart of existence. The lack of this understanding is the defilement to be overcome.

Pure knowing experience comes about by letting everything be in its reality of thusness; there is no need to add or remove anything. Even so-called defilements are already perfect defilements, so there is no necessity for transforming them. Just recognizing them for what they really are makes them disappear as what they really are not. The goal of contemplative exercise is the eradication of unwholesome seed impressions from the storehouse consciousness. These seeds are the base of subverting and hindering tendencies and proclivities. When attention is passive, not willfully active, these proclivities are allowed sanction to arise in the mind-stream of reactive thinking and behavior. Abandoning attachment to this passive process of automated reactivity is the practice, but this cannot be performed without first recognizing what is almost continually arising from the depths of alayavijnana. Passive attention must be remade into active vigilance. Actively vigilant, then distractions have no effect when they are recognized as thusness.

Presence is an active and willful silence of thusness. When presence is compromised, there is a slip back into a hypnotic passivity where automated reactivity of mental effluents can resume. The onlooker, stabilized in presence, can look on through the mind of thusness, with no preference, no prejudice, just *seeing* thusness. Hindering proclivities will gradually fade away due to this contemplative practice, a return to primal, free consciousness. Pure receptivity in pure presence is an open attentiveness, not to what was or to what might be, but to what is, here and now, with no particular fixation, just the free consciousness of the knowing onlooker.

Vigilantly receptive, waiting patiently for the next thought to manifest, then no thought will arise. This is the gap between thoughts. In this gap there is a mental silence with no words and no images disturbing or distracting pure presence. Mental functioning becomes quiescent. The gap will not last more than a few seconds at first, but those few seconds are enough to recognize what pure presence is. And it is a knowing awareness, not just a vacant reflector.

There are two fundamental ways that thoughts usually arise: as concepts described by words or as concepts portrayed as images. Images, mental pictures, are more subtle than discursive, word-laden ideas, but the practitioner progressively gets more and more acutely aware of these images. Both types of mentation are conceptual fabrications and when they are caught arising they are just dismissed as soon as one becomes aware of them. They then subside back into their source. This process is one of active and attentive detachment from rising thoughts, and with each practice session the seeds in the alayavijnana wither away more and more so that the mechanical arisings have less and less power to arise. The automatic and habitual mechanism of passive mentation and daydream imagery is thus slowly de-energized. The power of relaxed lucidity is all that is required and a sustained and stable presence in the gap between thoughts is possible.

No matter what kind of thought appears. Be aware of it as what-it-really-is, thusness, and let it go its own way; just let it go. Continue with diligence in attentive presence until attentive presence is the normal state of awareness at all times. This is the right kind of effort, but keep it relaxed. This kind of right effort is equated with proper discernment, or the ability to distinguish skillful from unskillful mental qualities. To be alert and vigilant means being clearly aware of what is happening in the present moment. Being mindful means to be able to remember to do this. The task is twofold: remaining focused on thusness and putting aside or dismissing all distractions. Just stay with immediate experience without slipping back into an automated mental narrative. Thus, one becomes more aware of the potential to slip back into distraction. This contemplation is a monitoring of attention, being alert and attentive to movements of attention.

All phenomenal events arise and pass away. External events and internal events, such as physical objects, mental objects, and events of attention are all temporal; they all come and they all go. Just be aware of them as thusness events and let them follow their natural course unimpeded. Watch for the factors which accompany them and lead to their origination and dissolution. This is the mind of thusness, and the more one can get stabilized in this attitude the more skillful mental qualities will be maximized. This must be mastered, rather than just being a complacent and passive witness. Thusness recognition is an acute sensitivity to conditionality. It is easy to just let things be thus.

Sensitivity to the present moment requires sufficient training in concentration. When a thought from the past or a thought for the future arises, it must simply be dismissed. Not that thoughts, or thinking, reflecting on past events, or thinking and planning for the future here are being relegated as worthless; they are not worthless. What is worthless and a waste of life is letting habitual mentation, like daydreams, take over the mind. Since we are heirs of our individual actions and thoughts, care should be taken to detach from worthless mental activity in every moment. Just keep the awareness of what is happening in the present moment, what the habit of the mind in the present moment seems to be. Being really in the present when mind finally settles down is an adjustment toward contemplative proficiency; this is the movement of prajna. But this does not mean that we will arrive at some projected goal at some future time. The present moment is already present; it only remains to stabilize awareness in this presence.

Dismissal of an arising thought is possible only after vigilance has waned and lucidity has been corrupted by falling back into distraction. In the absence of vigilant concentration, which permits a thought, and then a multitude of thoughts, to arise, only then can thoughts be dismissed. One merely remembers again that distraction has happened and then again distraction ends and vigilance is restored. This is the practice. When vigilance is restored, then thoughts can be dismissed. We are not trying to kill out all thoughts. Right thinking is necessary, but it is a willful activity of a properly discerning mind. What we are after is to eliminate habitual delusion based on errant discriminations. When habitual thoughts and daydreams start up again, just return to presence and dismiss them. This, done many, many times during the day, sets up a sort of alert system in the mind itself, the alert to awakening.

The vigilant sustaining of attentive presence is not another habit; it is the interruption or breaking down, breaking apart of the structures that sustain the automaton mind. Acute vigilance allows attention to remain active, falling not again back into passivity. So the practice of vigilant presence is concerned with the state of attention itself. Passivity of attention is inattentiveness, whereas active attention is willful direction of attention. Wakeful contemplatives monitor the status of their attention. When automated thoughts flow in the mind-stream then attentiveness has once again waned into passivity. The unbiased dismissal of automated thought is the disassembly of the proclivity patterns they exist in, and the re-activation of clarity, insight, and lucidity.

What it boils down to is whether or not we are distracted and dreaming. All the implications of distracted semi-awareness result in non-awakening, non-bodhi. So basically there is either distraction or there is awakening. The correct and most profound and efficient practice is the repeated recognition of distractedness, over and over until a subtle change in the awareness occurs, one that is overtly vigilant and actively attentive. Once this change becomes more and more continuous, then stability in the primal state of bodhi becomes securely established and distractedness becomes more and more absent.

The perfect and spontaneous recognition of thusness is the correct standpoint of practice. This naked awareness is called naked because it is not clothed with overlays and superimpositions made by mind. Superimpositionless awareness is that nondual apperception poised between Being and Becoming, the two truths. Being and Becoming are both facts and neither exists alone. Form and emptiness do not differ. Both are thusness and when seen and understood without delusion, overlays, or superimposed ideas – this is the samadhi of thusness. The only difference between a common person and a buddha is that the common person lives in a mind continually projecting and superimposing, not knowing his real condition. On the other hand, a buddha does not live subservient to a projecting and automaton reactive mind, and he knows his real condition, and he knows the real condition of the common person. He understands perfectly. The common person does not realize he is asleep and dreaming. A buddha knows he is awake and that the common man is asleep.

How does one get stabilized in the vision of thusness? There will, of necessity be a protracted ordeal because of habitual propensities and attachment to results, or to the fruit of practice. Ego-based motives are always concerned with the fruit. So we deceive ourselves until we can consciously be on guard against our base propensity, the ego-notion and the non-understanding of emptiness. Through study, thoughtful reflection, meditation, and certainty we can learn to *see* beyond ego and acknowledge the truth. All biased discriminations, like beautiful and ugly, vulgar and noble, fast and slow, pleasant and unpleasant, are perceptive distortions. The truth must be sought for behind whatever happens to be its transitory phenomenal expression.

Thus it is. The machine of karma is a spinning wheel of spatiotemporal conditioned causality, unrelenting, unyielding, and uncompromising.

Karma is also thusness; it is as-it-is. The only thing necessary to remember is to never be distracted. Keep checking to see if distraction has once again taken over; if it has, that's karma, that's thusness, that's how it is. Return to the mind of thusness, seeing the karmic cycles roll on and on. Just cease to get entangled in them. Recognize things as-they-really-are and recognize distractedness as habit-energy to be conquered. That is why the bodhisattva warrior is a warrior, and when having conquered, he is a conqueror, a tathagata, gone into, disappeared into thusness. This is bodhi svaha! Such it is.

The power and influence of karma and interdependent conditioned arising is a vast and complex cycle. The structure of the cycle points to its possible end. Karma causes birth into cyclic existence. Ignorance is the foundation for all false projections and errant discriminations; from these all kinds of conflict and afflictions arise. Conceptual thought structures are developed in the midst of all the errant mentations and delusions which sustain themselves and promote further delusion, particularly about the notions of intrinsic selfhood based on identification with the five skandhas, and on the presumed intrinsic existence of objective phenomena. When concepts based on errant discrimination cease through insight into emptiness, the whole karmic nexus is transcended and made impotent.

167

Understanding this sequence of the thusness of the matrix of existence, the process for conquering it can be fortuitously understood. Thus the samsaric cycle comes to rest.

"Sariputra, bodhisattva mahasattvas should train in the Profound Perfection of Wisdom in just this way."

"Bodhi Svaha!"

The End

Also by this author:

Gnosis

A Philosophical Psychology Concerning the Emergence of Individuated Holistic Intelligence

gnostiko.com

INDEX

Buddhadharma, 6, 24, 45, 57, 72, 80, 115

buddha-mind, 123

buddha-nature, 5, 102-103, 140, 142

Buddha (Sakyamuni), 2, 4, 5, 11, 24, 31-33, 37, 39, 43, 65, 76, 87, 90, 108, 110, 145

calm & insight, (see samatha-vipasyana), 17

cart simile, 51

causality, 126, 133, 166

certainty, ix, 18, 20-21, 25, 83, 117, 121, 123, 125-126, 129, 135, 151

chaos, ix

cinta, 20, 25

cintamayiprajna, 18, 20, 81

cittamatra, 5

clarity, vii

clinging, 49, 67, 103

clinging to practices, 26

compassion, 35, 147

concentration, 108-109, 111, 115

conceptual overlay (imputation), 59, 61, 140, 165

conditionality, 62, 64, 67-68, 74, 97, 100, 105, 117, 129, 139, 146-147, 154, 157, 162

conscioiusness, ix, 39, 49, 66

contact, 66

contemplation, 39

contemplating, contemplative, 3, 7, 18, 21, 36, 58, 94, 119, 133-134, 144, 149, 164

conqueror, 11, 14, 33, 87, 89-90, 167

siddhis, 43, 89

signless, 27

six perfections, 4, 27-28

six sense objects, 64-65

six sense organs (media), 63-66

skandhas, 11, 12, 15, 39, 41, 48-50, 53-54, 61, 63, 94, 131, 155, 167

smile, 25

sons and daughters, 11, 46

soul, 93, 96

spontaneous presence, 131

sravakas, 26

Srisimha, 6

srutamayiprajna, 17-18, 20, 81

sruti, 17

stages of the path, 34-35, 37

stopping and seeing (see samatha-vipasyana)

storehouse consciousness, 54, 83, 95, 159

stream-enterer, 26

study, 17

subtotality complex, 148

subtraction, 58

suffering, viii, ix, 8, 15, 40, 77-78, 93, 98, 108, 119, 135

sunyata (see emptiness), 3, 59, 92, 98-99, 132

superimposition, 117, 120, 130, 165

supramundane, 25-26, 121, 143-144

Sutta Pitaka, 4

truth, viii, 25, 75, 91, 102, 104-105, 118, 120, 122, 125, 128, 136, 154-155, 166

truth-vision, ix

twelve sense bases, 64-65

two truths, 5, 126-130, 134-135, 148, 154, 165

undersea city, 2

uniqueness, 148

unsurpassed, 27, 143-144

Vaipulya, 1

Vajrapani, 6

Vedic, 93

veil of ignorance, 28

venerable, venerated, 11, 14, 24, 44

Vimalamitra, 6

Vinaya Pitaka, 4

vipasyana (see samatha-vipasyana)

Visuddhimagga, 97

Vulture Mountain, 11, 33, 132

warrior saints, 17

waves and ocean simile, 142, 146

wholeness, 75, 148

wisdom, 1, 4, 7, 8, 17, 19, 27-29, 61, 82-83

wishless, 27

wrong beliefs, 75-76

wrong views, 58-59, 119

Yogacarya, 129

Zeus, 65

www.ingramcontent.com/pod-product-compliance
Lightning Source LLC
Chambersburg PA
CBHW070821100426
42813CB00003B/446